Mystery of Sin

Origin, Nature, Transmission, Effects, Consequences, Penalties, and Remedy

Wade H. Phillips

Mystery of Sin

Origin, Nature, Transmission, Effects, Consequences, Penalties, and Remedy

Published by Zion Assembly Church of God Publishing House
PO Box 2398
Cleveland, TN 37320-2398
USA
website: http://www.zionassemblychurchofgod.com

ISBN 13: 9781945622052
ISBN 10: 1945622059

Contents

Part III

Foreword

This book by Bishop Phillips is a timely answer to the popular view of sin being propagated in this generation---namely, that sin is an evil from which there is no full cure or deliverance in this present world, not even through the shed blood of Christ and His sanctifying grace. Accordingly, men are therefore never free from sin and its effects in this life, despite Jesus' declaration in Jn. 8:34-36 and the plain declarations of the apostles in the New Testament.

Bishop Phillips, with 50 years of ministerial experience as a pastor, evangelist, teacher, overseer, and presently as Presiding Bishop of Zion Assembly Church of God, is uniquely qualified to make such an important addition to the academic and theological writings available concerning sin. The *Mystery of Sin* not only explains the proper biblical view of sin but confronts head on many of the false teachings and misunderstandings of sin that are prevalent in our contemporary "Christian" world. In a time when classical Wesleyan-holiness doctrine is being brushed aside in favor of more sin-lenient interpretations, this book is a breath of fresh air. The *Mystery of Sin* treats the doctrine of sin from the perspectives of sin's origin, nature, transmission, effects, consequences, penalties and remedy. The confusion is thus dispelled to reveal the mystery of sin.

In a broader sense, Bishop Phillips' central thesis is a battle cry for a revival of true holiness, a call to renew doctrinal truth among

Christians and for increased desire to seek to understand sin and its remedy thru justification and the second definite work of grace, sanctification. It will be a standard text going forward for educating ministers and Christian workers about the doctrines related to sin. Whether in seminaries, Bible colleges, Sunday schools or personal devotions, the *Mystery of Sin* will help to keep Christians and local congregations rooted in biblical holiness. Further, I pray that this book will rekindle a desire to study and debate these important topics. The Christian world needs to come to grips with truth versus heresy in regard to sin.

The problem of sin must be acknowledged, confronted and dealt with. Through grace and faith, the sinner must repent and believe the Gospel: receive Christ into his heart, turn away from sin and bow to the lordship of Christ in obedience to His commandments. God has provided the means in Christ for believers to live victoriously over sin. Of course, victory will not be won if Christians continue to doubt and discount the works of God. Believers must accept by faith the plain truths of the Holy Scriptures and turn away from false teachings.

God is preparing His Bride. He is calling Christians out of denominations and independent ministries into one-fold, into one universal body of Christ. Correct doctrine helps to identify the true church and pave the way toward that prophetic goal. This book on sin is one way in which the church is fighting the good fight of faith, by calling Christians out of religious confusion and false teachings and back to their first love: a true and affectionate relationship with Christ and His Word. We may rest assured that God's people will be one upon Christ's return, and *"without spot or wrinkle or any such thing"* (Jn. 10.16; Eph. 1.10; 4.11-16; 5.27).

Anton Burnette
Director of Education
Zion Assembly Church of God

Part 1

Introduction

Sin is plainly revealed in the Bible: yet the full scope of its nature and characteristics is not neatly defined and packaged in a specific formula; rather, it is understood and seen for what it is through a variety of ways and mediums:

1. by the revelation of God in nature (Ps. 19.1-9; Acts 17.24-30; Rom. 1.20; 10.18-20; 1 Cor. 11.14-15).

2. by the revelation of God's law in Holy Scripture (Rom. 3.20; 4.15; 5.20; 7.7-13) which is understood especially in the light of the teachings of Christ and the apostles in the New Testament (Mt. 5.20-48; 6.1-34; 7.24; Acts 2.22-37; Eph. 3.3-5; 4.17-32; 5.1-7).

3. by the convicting power of the Holy Spirit (Mt. 12.31-32; Jn. 16.7-15; Acts 7.51-55; Rom. 8:1-11, 13-16; see also Gen. 6.3; Ps. 51.10-11).

4. by the moral law of God written in human consciousness, which speaks to men authoritatively, rendering them without excuse for their rebellious acts (Rom. 1.19-20).

5. by the testimonies of born-again believers who have overcome sin; by the embodiment of God manifested in the lives of His people (Mt. 5.14-16; 2 Cor. 3.2-3) whose light shines forth in holiness and practical righteousness, thereby exposing by contrast the darkness of sin; and, finally, by the discerning judgments that operate as a gift in His church (Is. 35.8; Mt. 5.13-16;16.19; 18.15-20; Jn. 20.23; Acts 5.1-11; 1 Cor. 5.1-13; 6.1-5; 2 Cor. 3.2-3; Eph. 3.9, 10; 5.8-13; 1 Tim. 3.15; et al).

Still, sin is a mystery in many respects. It is like certain mysteries we see in nature. Agur wrote: *"There are three things which are too wonderful for me, Four which I know not [do not understand]: The way of an eagle in the air; the way of a serpent upon a rock; the way of a ship in the midst of the sea; and the way of a man with a maid"* (Prov. 30.18-20). Sin is thus referred to as the *"mystery of iniquity"* (2 Thess. 2.7; see also 1 Sam. 15.23; Ps. 51.5; Jer. 17.9); for there is a degree of mystery in the origin of sin, both in angelic and human experience; in its transmission through Adam to his posterity; in its nature and effects; and in the unfathomable depths of its evil potential.

Some questions about sin have never been satisfactorily answered, and we do not pretend here to fully solve every mystery in this small book, nor to give a definitive answer to every question regarding the subject. Some things are known only to God and must remain hidden in Him (Job 11.7; Rom. 11.33). *"For now we see through a glass [mirror], darkly; but then face to face: now I know in part; but then shall I know even as also I am known"* (1 Cor. 13.9-12). Thus, we are admonished by the apostle to avoid theological hair-splitting and vain speculations (1 Tim. 1.4; 6.3-5; 2 Tim. 2.16, 23; Titus 3.9-11). Regarding the mysteries that are too high for us, we simply stand before the throne of His Majesty and worship, admiring and resting in faith in the Lord's infinite wisdom and power.

Our task here then is to focus on what the Scriptures plainly teach about sin, comparing scripture with scripture, employing the powers of reason, and judging our common experiences to set forth the nature and effects of this deadly disease of the soul, and God's remedy for it in Christ. Accordingly, we will deal with the subject somewhat comprehensively, though not exhaustively, and will endeavor to make each point consistent with every other point.

Origin of Sin

Sin is neither an illusion in the mind, nor merely the absence of good; it is rather a real and dynamic force in the world, a spirit that runs contrary to the will of God. It is not eternal, and thus did not exist in the beginning with good. The idea that good and evil are eternally co-existent is a pagan notion ("dualism"), not a biblical truth.[1] For God in the beginning created everything *"very good"* (Gen. 1.31).

---

[1] The damaging heresy of dualism troubled the church in the early centuries. Multitudes of believers were swept into the currents created by certain Gnostic sects. The teachings of a radical offshoot of Gnosticism known as Manichaeism found their way into Christian thinking in the late fourth- and early fifth century through Augustine, and later through John Calvin *via* the writings of Augustine.

Sin and evil came into being and appeared in the world as a corruption of the good. It found expression first in the personality and will of Satan, the "father of lies" (Is. 14.12-14; Ezek. 28.15; Jn. 8.44; 1 Jn. 3.8). Apparently, when Lucifer said, "I will," with the intent to disobey and defy God, sin began (Is. 14.12; see also Ezek. 28.15). Lucifer thereupon became *Satan,* a name which in Hebrew means "adversary" and/or "false accuser," a fitting title for one who opposes both God and man. *Devil* means "slanderer" and "accuser", thus, the two names---*Satan* and *Devil*---are used together in Rev. 12.9 to identify Lucifer.

Sin originated in man in the paradise of Eden when Adam and Eve, under the crafty influence and temptation of Satan, rebelled against the commandment of God and ate of the forbidden fruit (Gen. 3.6, 17; contrast with Eccl. 7.29; see also 1 Tim. 2.13-14). In Gen. 3.1-7 we are shown that our first parents came under the influence of Satan and began to doubt the Word of God and became confused. Satan tricked them. They then turned their attention from the *"tree of life"* to focus on the "forbidden tree." This resulted in unbelief and apostasy---Adam and Eve *"departed from the faith."* Under satanic delusion, they blindly chose death over life! (1 Cor. 4.4).

The origin of sin in man therefore cannot be blamed on Satan altogether; in fact, the Lord puts the primary blame on the man himself. Adam acted finally from a selfish motive, and for a self-serving purpose. In his capacity as a free moral agent---having been created in the image of God---he was thus endowed with the power of free will and independent action, and, as such, yielded to the evil principle suggested by Satan and became a victim of the *"spirit of disobedience."* He acted from a free moral agency, and thus chose the path of defiance and rebellion. The first man acted in a self-assertive manner, exalting himself over against the will and preeminence of God. He became arrogant and egotistical. The rebellious "I will" that caused the fall of Satan (Is. 14.12-14; Lu. 10.18; Rev. 12.9, 13), was reenacted in the heart and rebellious act of Adam. In effect, Adam said, "Not Thy will but mine be done!"

Further, being the natural head of the race, the sin nature was transmitted through Adam to the whole race, that is, the nature of sin and its penalty---namely, *"death through sin"* was transmitted to *"all men"* (Rom. 5.12). Like Christ, the "second Adam" (v. 14; see also 1 Cor. 15.45-49), the actions of the first Adam had a universal significance for all of humanity; for all men have inherited a depraved nature from him.

It is precisely on this point---on original sin and how it is transmitted, and its consequences---that many speculations and false teachings have their origin and grounding, beginning most significantly in the Roman Catholic Church in the late fourth century with the arguments between Pelagius (c.360-c.420) and his contemporary, Augustine of Hippo (354-430). Generally-speaking, believers are separated into three camps in respect to the way original sin is perceived, namely:

1. **the Pelagian tradition,** named for Pelagius, a British or Irish monk who theologized the system in the fourth century[2]. This system: *a)* maintained man's free agency and a liberal view of divine grace; *b)* denied original sin and total depravity; *c)* denied the original immortality of Adam and human kind; and *d)* held that Adam and his posterity did not sustain any moral injury by his disobedience.

2. **the Augustinian-Calvinistic tradition**, named for Augustine of Hippo and John Calvin. This system: *a)*

---

[2] There is some evidence that suggests one Rufinus, "the Syrian", assisted in theologizing the Pelagian system. Adrian Hastings, ed. *The Oxford Companion to Christian Thought* (Oxford: University Press, 2000), pp. 526-527.

maintained original sin and total depravity; *b)* added, however, a body of doctrine to these truths that was unscriptural and heretical, including an extreme view of God's sovereignty over against, and at the expense of, man's free agency; *c)* developed an elaborate theological system that failed to balance the grace of God and the atonement of Christ against the fall of man, and thus created a system of moral paralysis and despair.

3. **the Arminian-Wesleyan tradition**, named for Jacob Arminius and John Wesley. This system: *a)* agreed in some respects with the Augustinian-Calvinistic tradition, including total depravity as a result of Adam's fall, with the result of condemnation and punishment upon the whole race; *b)* agreed with the Pelagian system in regard to the free agency of man; *c)* and most significantly and admirably balanced the fall of man with the universal grace of God and the atonement of Christ. This system thus acknowledged total depravity and its devastating consequences but focused rather on the eternal decree of Christ's atoning sacrifice, and the universal grace and mercy of God, showing that the principles of the Gospel were readily available in Eden even while the fall was then in motion, for the Gospel is the *free gift* of God's grace to save and redeem Adam and Eve and their posterity.[3]

The impact of these three traditions on the development of denominational divisions and various doctrinal systems will be

---

[3] Wesley's views on original sin and its consequences and remedy are laid out at length in his 1756 work, *The Doctrine of Original Sin: According to Scripture, Reason, and Experience* (Nicholasville, KY: Schmul Publishing Co., 1999, reprint).

elaborated upon further ahead. Suffice it to say here that Zion Assembly agrees basically with the Arminian-Wesleyan view.

The Soul of Man---the Seat of Sin

Man is a trichotomy, constituted of spirit, soul, and body (1 Thess. 5.23; Heb. 4.12). However, there is a thin line of distinction between the spirit and soul, the very depths of the nature and mystery of which lie beyond human understanding (cp. Gen. 2.7 with Heb. 4.12). Many scholars believe the soul and spirit are the same; but we see in Scripture clear evidence of the tri-substance of man's nature. Even so, we see no benefit here to argue the point at any length. Suffice it to say that though man is represented as being constituted of three substances, yet his spirit and soul seem to be simply two sides of the immaterial nature of man in distinction from his body.[4]

The soul and spirit are thus inseparable, even in death. The two substances pervade and interpenetrate each other.[5] The Greek terms *psyche* ["soul"] and *pneuma* ["spirit"] are thus often used synonymously or interchangeably in distinction from the *soma* ["body"] (Eccl. 12.7; Rev. 6.9-10; Mt. 10.28; Jas. 2.26). Notwithstanding, the Bible is replete with references to the distinctions between the soul and spirit, and the need to maintain them. The basic distinction seems to be that the spirit represents the higher nature of man's immaterial part connected with his image and likeness to God, and as such having the potential for worship, prayer, and spirituality, and contrariwise the potential to

---

[4] A.H. Strong, *Systematic Theology*, (Valley Forge, PA: Judson Press, 1907), p. 484.

[5] Myer Pearlman, *Knowing the Doctrines of the Bible* (Springfield, MO: Gospel Publishing House, 1937), pp 106-108.

defy God. Thus, a man may have a *"haughty spirit"* (Prov. 16.18; also 2 Cor. 7.1) or a *"contrite and humble spirit"* (Is. 57.15; Mt. 5.3); whereas the soul is more clearly connected with the inferior bodily senses (sight, hearing, taste, smell, touch), which serve as the soul's agents to intercommunicate with the material world around it.[6]

Animals too are endowed with some type of life principle, which in the original Hebrew text is called a "soul" in Gen. 1.20. It is the same word used for the soul of man in vv. 26-27; both are thus translated *psyche* in the Greek Septuagint version of the Old Testament. Elsewhere, however, the distinction between the soul of man and animal life is made perfectly clear. Men are immortal persons, animals are not persons and thus cease to exist at death. Note that at death the bodies of men like the bodies of animals return to dust (Eccl. 3.18-20); but the *spirit* as well as the soul of man goes upward, back to God who gave it; but the spirit of animals goes back to dust in the earth and ceases to be (v. 21; see also Eccl. 12.7; 2 Cor. 5.6-8). It is thus that the spirit and soul of man make him different from all other creatures.

All human flesh therefore has a God-given spirit and soul in individual form (Num. 16.22; 27.16). In distinction from animals, the human spirit and soul give man God-consciousness and God-likeness. The soul of man came into existence in the beginning by

---

[6] Both the soul and spirit can spiritually die within a living physical body; yet in physical death the spirit and soul are separated from the body (2 Cor. 5.8); further, the soul and spirit immediately upon death go back to God and enter into a state of joy if the person's name is written in the book of life (Eccl. 12.7; Rev. 13.8; 17.8); or otherwise into a state of torment if his name is not in the book (Lu. 16.19-31; Rev. 20.12). Meanwhile the bodies of both the saint and the sinner decay in their earthly graves awaiting their respective resurrections (Acts 24.15): the righteous await the glorious first resurrection, the rapture (Jn. 5.28-29; 1 Cor. 15.12-23, 41-58; 1 Thess. 4.16-18; Rev. 20.12), the rest await the resurrection of the damned following the Millennial Reign (Rev. 20.12; see also Mt. 25.46).

the supernatural breath of God. Adam thereby became a *"living soul" [or "living being"]* (Gen. 1.26-27; 2.7). Thus, the soul is the very seat of man's life---the intelligent life principle that animates his bodily organs and senses for self-expression and objective communications with the world around it. It is the seat of his rationality and his knowledge of God; and the basis of his distinction as an individual, that is, the soul distinguishes one person from another. It is thus that "souls" are often equated with "persons" in Scripture (Ex. 1.5; Rom. 13.1).[7]

The soul of man distinguishes him from animals on one hand, and from angels on the other: for angels do not have souls nor physical bodies. Angels are called *"spirits"* in Heb. 1.14 but are nowhere called souls: and, without physical bodies, they are not subject to material laws and conditions. For the same reason, God is called a *"Spirit"* (Jn. 4.24)[8], though He is uncreated, eternal, and infinite, whereas angels are created beings and finite. Man is therefore distinguished as a "soul in a body".

"The Word of God is in the Bible as the soul is in the body"
---Peter Taylor Forsyth

There are two theories of how human souls have come into existence since Adam that are worthy of our attention. The *Creation theory* states that each soul is created by the Lord at conception; the *Traducian theory* states that the soul is transmitted from the parents to the infant by natural generation. The Traducian

---

[7] Merrill C. Tenney, gen. ed., *The Zondervan Pictorial Encyclopedia of the Bible*, 5 Vols. (Grand Raids: Zondervan Publishing House, 1975), V, pp. 496-498; Ronald F. Youngblood, gen. ed., *New Illustrated Bible Dictionary* (Nashville: Thomas Nelson Publishers, 1995), pp. 1195, 1196.

[8] It is noteworthy that the article "a" is not in the original Greek text; thus *"God is Spirit"* is the preferred rendering: a point noticed in the NKJV and NASV and other translations.

theory seems most in accord with the Scriptures and reason: for original sin which is seated in the soul is passed on through natural generation, and parental characteristics are also transmitted to the offspring through natural generation. Note also the apparent Scriptural support: Gen. 5.3; Job 10.8-12; Ps. 139.14-16; Eccl. 11.5; Jn. 1.13; 3.6; Rom. 5.12; 1 Cor. 15.22; Eph. 2.3; Heb. 7.9-10; et al. We do not deny the possibility, however, that God may work in some miraculous or supernatural way with the parents in the creation or procreation of the soul (see footnotes 6 and 12 below for further explanation).

In either case, the soul is the very seat of man's life, including his natural instincts and the driving forces of his personality---his intelligence, will, and emotions.[9] We might say that the mind is the "soul thinking", the body is the "soul feeling", the will is the "soul choosing."[10] The soul is our "self", our "inner man". It permeates and inhabits every part of the body; thus, the soul is described often as performing bodily acts (Gen. 44.30; Lev. 5.1-2; Prov. 13.4; Is. 32.6; Jer. 16.16; Ezek. 23.17, 22; et al). The body is therefore the instrument of the soul; the soul is the *ego* or "I" of the person acting through the body to fulfill its will and desires.

The soul is thus also the seat of sin. For every sin that a man commits is *"without the body"* (1 Cor. 6.18), which may mean in one sense that sin originates in the spirit and soul, not the body, the body being merely the instrument for the will and affections of the soul, the self. Thus, *"the soul that [sins] it shall die"* (Ezek. 18.4, 20), and again, *"If a soul shall sin . . ."* (Lev. 4.2). Notwithstanding, the "heart" and "mind" are often equated with the soul in Scripture and described as the seat of good and/or of

---

[9] Pearlman, *Knowing the Doctrines of the Bible*, pp. 103-112.

[10] Strong, *Systematic Theology*, pp. 488-497.

evil in man. Thus, Jesus, *"A good man out of the good treasure of his heart [brings] forth that which is good; and an evil man out of the evil treasure of his heart [brings] forth that which is evil: for of the abundance of the heart his mouth [speaks]"* (Lu. 6.45; see also Mt. 12.34-35).

Essence of Sin

The spirit of "I will" over against the Will of God is the very core of sin. This disposition in man is arrogant and self-serving; it indicates supreme love for oneself over against loving God supremely. Thus, one of the primary characteristics of sin is self-assertive egotism, which is closely related to pride. Making a play on the English word **SIN**, someone has thus pointed out that the middle letter is **"I"**.

Sin is willful rebellion against God and His law (Ps. 51.3-4; Luke 12:47-48; Heb. 4.7; 10.26; 13.18; 2 Pet. 3.5)[11]. It may be expressed in the form of *lawlessness* (Rom. 3.20; 4.15; 5.13; Gal. 3.19; 1 Tim. 1.9), *transgression* (Ps. 119.158; Eph. 2.1; 1 Jn. 3.4), *disobedience* (Rom. 8.7; Titus 1.16; 3.3; 1 Tim. 1.9; 1 Pet. 2.7-8), *pride/conceit* (Job 41.34; Ps. 59.12; Prov. 16:18; Is. 14.12-14; Ezek. 28.15; 1 Jn. 2.16), *rebellion* (Ps. 78.8; Lam. 1.18;; Dan. 9.5), *sensuality* (Jas. 3.15; Jude 19), and *unbelief* (Jn. 3.18; Titus 1.15; 1 Jn. 2.22-24; Rev. 21.8).

The sin of unbelief is rooted and manifested in prideful rebellion, that is, in personal defiance against the glory, sovereignty, and character of God (Gen. 3.5-6; Job 41.34; Prov. 11.2; 13.10; 16.18; 29.23; Is. 14.12-14; Jer. 13.9; 49.16; 1 Tim.

---

[11] We do not deny, however, that some sins that may lie below consciousness; or otherwise are committed in ignorance or unintentionally.

3.6; 1 Jn. 2.16). Adam and Eve, under the deceptive influence of Satan, first doubted God, then denied His truth, authority, and majestic character; and finally exalted themselves to a status of self-serving autonomy. They made themselves their own masters, and thus deprived God of His lordship!

Every sinner does the same: he denies or resists the convicting power of the Holy Spirit, who reveals God's truth in Christ, including His sovereign will and majestic glory (Jn. 15:26; 16.7-15; 17.1-26). Moreover, in the place of Christ, the sinner exalts himself, which becomes a form of idolatry. In this way, the first and greatest commandment---to love God supremely (Mt. 22.37-40), is broken by every man who comes into the world (Rom. 3.23). This is the very heart of sin and the primary motive in disobedience, namely, self-exaltation and prideful autonomy.

Specific Words for Sin

There are several words in the Greek New Testament that help to define and explain the brevity of sin and its mystery. The most common is **hamartia**. This word means to "miss the mark," conveying the image of an archer who misses his target. But the original significance of the term has been largely lost in current thought. The ancients used it to denote not only failure to comply with God's will and purpose, but a willful defiance to go in a different direction---away from God. In other words, *hamartia* signifies the purposive turning away or going astray from God and His commandments. Yet in some instances it denotes *deviation* in distinction from outright defiance and rebellion. Further, *hamartia* refers to sin as both a state and an act (cp. Rom. 3.9-20; 6.6; 1 Jn. 3.4-5 with Mt. 9.6; 1 Jn. 3.8). It represents essentially the governing principle of sin, *"the body of sin", "the flesh"* (Rom.

6.6; Gal. 5.16-17, 19-21), that is, the underlying power of the depraved nature that inclines man to commit actual sins. It may exist in this state of being therefore below consciousness in the form of evil desires and passions and egotism, even in infants. All outward acts of sin in fact originate from this deeper disposition of sinfulness in the soul and spirit of man, that is, in native depravity.

Another prominent word for sin is **parabasis**. This term signifies the act of transgression. *"Where there is no law there is no transgression"* (Rom. 4.15); sin is therefore the breaking of the law of God---a law which speaks to man as an "imperative command." This command exists and acts through nature in man's moral consciousness. It was in this way that sin originated in man hundreds of years before the law of God was written in Scripture. Adam broke the expressed commandment of God and ate of the forbidden tree (Gen. 2.17). Observe, Adam and Eve did not merely deviate from the commandment of God, they defied it! **Parabasis** therefore conveys the idea that men consciously and willfully rebel against the law of God. Thus, transgression cannot be relegated to a mere mistake or mental error. Isaiah captured the essence of sin in this sense: *"As for our iniquities, we know them: in transgressing and lying against the LORD . . . Conceiving and uttering from the heart words of falsehood"* (Is. 59.12, 13).

Another term used often for sin is **asebeia**, which carries the idea of "ungodliness", that is, of being "impious" and "wicked", and thus unlike God. It denotes that the guilty party does not have a personal relationship with God. An ungodly person may know *about God* yet *not know God,* that is, he refuses to repent and be reconciled with God and to conform his life to God's life (Rom. 1.21). This form of sin leads to other sins, which in turn plunge man ever deeper into darkness and moral degradation (vv. 21-32).

Other words used for sin are **adikia**, "unrighteousness" (Lu. 16.6; Acts 18.14); **anomia**, "lawlessness" (Mt. 7.23; Rom. 4.7;

1 Jn. 3.7); *poneria*, "malicious evil" (Mk. 7.22; Eph. 6.12); *epithymia*, "evil lust, desire" (Mk. 4.19; Lu. 22.15); *hedone*, "excess, unbridled, unsanctified pleasure" (Jas. 4.1-3).

An Ugly Portrait

All of the words just noticed, and their derivatives, carry the ideas of perversion, idolatry, sorcery, divination, deceit, conceit, worldliness, impiety, hypocrisy, evil passions, lusts, lying, stealing, falsity of all kinds, confusion, moral disorders of all kinds, emulation, strife, division, contentions, sedition, hatred, bitterness, anger, vengeance, spite, wrath, malicious quarrels, murder, slander, evil and injurious speaking of all kinds, uncleanness, fornication, adultery, homosexuality, bestiality, lewdness, lasciviousness, licentiousness, concupiscence and works of the flesh of all kinds---malice, envy, jealousy, greed, extortion, drunkenness, gluttony, revelry, and fleshly corruptions of every stripe. Together, these words paint a comprehensive portrait of *sin*, revealing it in its many despicable expressions and manifestations. They show that sin is a deadly cancer of the soul; a disease of the human spirit; moral and spiritual filth; stench; pollution; carnality. Sin is thus ugly and demeaning; reproachful to God and man; offensive to grace and reason; an insult to dignity; and a contradiction of love and goodness. In a word, sin is the spirit of error, the spirit of disobedience; an evil, loathsome, putrefying corruption of the heart and soul.

The substance of sin is *"earthly, sensual, devilish"* (Jas. 3.15), and its manifestations are an outrage against the holiness, goodness, and the charitableness of God. It is mockery of God and man: for man was created in God's image and exists to *"show forth his praises"* (1 Pet. 2.9). Sin repels and disgusts the Holy Spirit and is also abhorrent to every child of God filled with His Spirit (Gen. 6.5-7; Ps. 101.3-8; Prov. 6.16-19; Is. 59.2-23, 18; Jn. 16.7-11; Rom. 1.18-32; 8.1-6). For *"sin is a reproach to any people"* (Prov. 14.34).

Seeing sin for what it is in the light of God's Word, and knowing God's wrath and judgment against it, prompted Peter to ask the rhetorical question: *"What manner of persons ought you to be in all holy conversation and godliness?"* (2 Pet. 3.11); which he then answered by referring to the Old Testament command, *"Be ye holy; for I am holy"* and his further admonition, *"be holy in all manner of conversation"* [conduct] (1 Pet. 1.15-16). Thus, Paul says, *"See then that you walk circumspectly . . . redeeming the time, because the days are evil"* (Eph. 5.15-16). In other words, we should walk carefully before the Lord, keeping ourselves *"unspotted from the world"* (Jas. 1.27), and to give all diligence to guard every aspect of our lives to please the Lord and to honorably represent Him as His ambassadors in this present world (2 Cor. 5.20). *"Stand in awe, and sin not: commune with your own heart. . . and be still. Selah"* (Ps. 4.4).

Heaven is a holy place,
Filled with glory and grace,
Sin can never enter there;
All within its gates are pure,
So, if at the judgment bar,
sinful spots your soul shall mar,
You can never enter there.

Sin Defined

The Scriptures explain sin in perspective of the relationship between the creature and his Creator. Thus, wherever and whenever a person volitionally separates himself from God and resists and rebels against His grace and expressed will, there is sin. Sin is therefore primarily the breach of a right relationship with God, both in the sense of inherited alienation caused by the fall of Adam and by willful separation through personal, actual sin. The breach of a right relationship between God and man in turn causes the violator to sin against his neighbor and against himself.

Sin may be expressed in *thought* (1 Jn. 3.15), *word* (Mt. 5.22), and/or *deed* (Rom. 1.32), and is committed either by omission or commission; the former by willfully ignoring what God has commanded, the latter by willfully doing what He has expressly forbidden. Sin is centered in the will and affections of man, not in his physical body, though the body is the organic instrument for the expression of sin (Rom. 6.12-14). Thus *"Every sin that a man does is without the body, but he that commits fornication sins against his own body"* (1 Cor. 6.18). Sin originates in the "heart", or soul, that is, in the seat of our affections and will (Mt. 15:17-20), and acts through the members of the body (Rom. 1.24; 6.11-13). Therefore, if sin exists in the heart, though it is not acted out, the person harboring it will incur psychological and spiritual damage. And this inbred sin acted out in deeds finally ends in eternal death and damnation (Ezek. 18.4; Mt. 5.21-28; Rom. 5.12-14, 17, 21; 6.23; Jas. 1.5).

Sin exists therefore not merely in the act of the sinner, but at a deeper level as a state of the soul. This sinfulness is called birth [native] depravity or original sin which all men inherit as children of Adam (Rom. 5.12-14; Eph. 2.2-3). This will be elaborated upon more fully in a moment.

The nature of sin, like the astrophysicist's image of a "black hole," is a powerful force that is ever spiraling downward into disorder and confusion; and we see in Scripture, history, and human experience that there seems to be no bottom to how low men will go under the influence of sin and evil. They can degenerate so far to mutate morally and spiritually into the likeness of *"brute beasts"* (1 Cor. 15.32; 2 Pet. 2.12; Jude 10). *"And, moreover, I saw under the sun the place of judgment, that wickedness was there; and . . . iniquity was there . . . I said in mine heart concerning the estate of the sons of men, that God might manifest them, and that they might see that they themselves are beasts"* (Eccl. 3.16-18). In God's judgment against Nebuchadnezzar, the king even mutated into the physical characteristics and habits of a beast: *"he was driven from men and ate grass like oxen, and his body was wet with the dew of heaven, till his hairs had grown like eagles' feathers and his nails like birds' claws"* (Dan. 4.33).

The natural tendency of sin, like that of the devil, is to kill, steal, and destroy. It is therefore never neutral; it is rather a real and effectual evil force that separates man from a holy God (Is. 59:2), pulling him down against the grace of Christ into an abyss of darkness, disorder, and despair. Thus, we see that rebellious Jonah went *"down"* to Joppa; *"down"* to the ship; *"down"* into the sides of the ship; and when cast out of the great fish's belly, he went *"down"* to the bottoms of the sea before being finally delivered (Jonah 1.3; 2.5-6).

Sin is an affront to God's character, and thus offensive to Him. He abhors sin! Hence the inspired prophet, *"Your iniquities have separated you from your God"* (Is. 59.2). God will not give an inch to sin. He cannot: for He is holy and just. Light has no fellowship with darkness; neither truth with deception; nor justice with wickedness and rebellion (2 Cor. 6.14-16; Eph. 5.11; 1 Jn. 1.6-7). It is thus that God *"will not at all acquit the wicked"* (Nah. 1.3). The apostle therefore describes sinners as the enemies of God (Rom. 5.10; Eph. 2.3). God hates sin and will have no fellowship with it (Heb. 1.9; Rev. 2.6). Though He loves the sinner, He must finally destroy him if he harbors and clings to his sin (Rom. 1.21-32; 1 Cor. 10.1-10; Heb. 10.26-29). The saying "turn or burn" is therefore appropriate: for if the sinner does not turn to Christ in faith and repentance, he will surely burn in hell forever (Mk. 9.43-48; Lu. 12.16-21; 16.19-31; Jn. 3.36; Gal. 6.6-7).

Sin breaks our fellowship with God and with our neighbors, and in that order; for we first sin against God, and this causes us to sin against others. David thus anchored his sins against Uriah and Bathsheba in his sin against God (2 Sam. 12.13; Ps. 51.4). Indeed, sin strikes out against God, defies Him! However, it is often concealed within the heart, hidden under a cloak of pretense, hypocrisy, and self-deception. This is what we see in Adam and Eve in Eden: an evil principle, a deceptive force captured the imagination of our first parents (Gen. 3.6; 6.5; 2 Cor. 10.5; 1 Tim. 2.14-16), and then moved them to reject God as the Lord and center of their lives; which in turn moved them to exalt themselves in His place---to usurp His authority in self-asserting autonomy. Satan deceived Eve into thinking that God is a liar and that she and Adam could be exalted on a plain equal with God. Recall that this was the very sin of Satan: *"I will be like the Most High"* (Is. 14.14).

Sin Illustrated

The seductive idea that gained Eve's attention was Satan's wily assertion, *"your eyes shall be opened, and you shall be as gods",* that is, *"you shall be like God"* (Gen. 3.5). Yielding to the temptation, Eve then implicated Adam, and they conspired together against God and His commandment. At that moment, they were *"far off"* from God, with *"no hope and without God in the world"* (Eph. 2.12-13). They had forsaken *life* to pursue *light!*

Significantly Eve was deceived; whereas Adam more consciously and deliberately rebelled against the commandment of God (1 Tim. 2.13-14). Sin was thus more particularly passed on to all men through Adam (Rom. 5.12, 15-19).

It is not without significance that the same motive and pattern of behavior that moved Satan and the angels to sin against God also moved Adam and Eve: namely, the pride of life and a self-centered and self-serving spirit, all of which possessed Eve and Adam before they ate the forbidden fruit (Gen. 3.6-7), that is, they first opened their heart to sin and evil, then acted it out. The apostle John seems to have had Adam and Eve and their rebellion in mind in summing up the essential aspects of sin: *"Love not the world, neither the things of the world . . . For all that is in world, the lust of the flesh, and the lust of the eyes, and the pride of life, is not of the Father, but of the world"* (1 Jn. 2.15-16). Adam and Eve thus fell from their "first estate" the same as the angels had before them, and for the same reasons and by the same means, namely, satanic deception, pride, evil desire, rebellion, and willful disobedience (cf. 2 Cor. 11.14-15; 2 Pet. 2.4; Jude 6; Rev. 12.3-12).

The kings of Tyre and Babylon and their kingdoms are used in Scripture to typify Satan and his rebellious followers (Is. 14.12-14; Ezek. 28.12-19; Rev. 12.3-12). But the fall of man, unlike the fall of Satan and the wicked angels, had special implications for redemption and God's glory: for man, not angels, was created in the image of God; and, unlike the angels, mankind is a race; thus, accordingly, sin is transmitted through human procreation.[12] On the positive side of this mystery, however, men can repent and be reconciled to God; whereas the wicked angels cannot, and thus, accordingly, the fallen angels have been eternally damned and consigned to the lake of fire (Rev. 12.9; 20.2-3, 10).

Transmission of Sin

Because mankind is a race, the nature of depravity or "original sin" has been transmitted to all men through the fall of the first man, Adam (Rom. 5.12-14, 17, 19; 1 Cor. 15.22).[13] Thus the term "racial sin". Accordingly, all men since the fall have been born naturally of a *"corruptible seed"* (1 Pet. 1.23). Men are *"conceived in sin"* (Ps. 51.5); *"The wicked are estranged from the womb"* (Ps. 58.3). Sin is therefore universal, because all men, constituted a race in Adam, are somehow implicated in the fall and thus identified with Adam. All men are consequently born with the nature of depravity (Gal. 3.22; Eph. 2.3; 1 Jn. 1.8). This is difficult to grasp

---

[12] On the origin of the soul and how sin is transmitted from generation to generation, *the Traducian theory* over against the *Creation theory* seems more plausible and in line with Scripture. The former holds that the soul comes into existence the same as the body---through procreation, i.e., natural generation; the latter theory states that each soul is created by God in the moment of conception; accordingly, the parents procreate only the body of the child. A third theory of the origin of the soul must be categorically rejected; namely, that all souls preexisted before they were conceived in the womb. This notion is simply old paganism couched in "Christian" pretense, represented anciently in Plato and Greek philosophy, later in Gnosticism and Manichaeism, all of which influenced some of the Early Church Fathers [Origen, e.g.]. More recently the pagan idea of the preexistence of souls has surfaced again in Mormonism and some New Age movements.

[13] We do not see the benefit here of caviling over the subtle distinctions and sophisticated arguments made by theologians between what is termed by some as "native [birth] depravity" and others as "original sin." In this book the terms are used synonymously.

and, admittedly, not fully comprehensible: but it is the only adequate explanation for the universality of sin. [14] Sin exists therefore not only universally in the acts of men but in a common depravity, the latter becoming manifest in the acts of men.

Accordingly, all men are born sinners in the sense that they are born in depravity. This innate sinfulness is denominated by the apostle as the *"body of sin"* and *"the flesh"* (Rom. 6.6; Col. 2.11; Gal. 5.16-17, 19-21), for it has infected every facet of man's personhood---soul, will, affections, intellect. All persons have thus inherited by natural birth this one body of sin. It may be said, therefore, that Adam as a person corrupted human nature; since Adam, human nature has corrupted every person.

This sinful nature is called *"the"* body of sin, not "a" body of sin, because all men share in this one universal body of sin. It is referred to as the *"body of sin"* also perhaps because the physical body is the organic instrument for it. In any case, we are admonished to receive Christ and become a new creature in Him so that we might be able to *"present [our] bodies a living sacrifice, holy, acceptable unto God . . ."* (Rom. 12.1). Another way of stating this mystery is that this body of sin is the root of the tree, to which the axe must be laid (Mt. 3.10); that is, if men desire to be made truly free, they must be delivered from and cleansed of this original body of sin.

To understand the nature of this body of depravity more insightfully, the apostle Paul personifies it as the *"old man,"* in contrast with the *"new man"* in Christ (Eph. 4.22-24; Col. 3.10). It is fallen Adam in contrast with Christ, the new Adam (Rom. 5.14-17; 1 Cor. 15.45-49). Again, it is not *an* old man, but *the* old man: for all men share in the original "old man", that is, the body

---

[14] John Miley, *Systematic Theology*, 2 Vols. (New York: Eaton and Mains, 1894), I, pp.463-464.

of sin inherited by all men through the fall of Adam. The term "Adamic nature" was thus coined to denote the inherited sinful nature. Note also Paul's image is designated the "old man," not "old men": for, again, all men since the fall are born of the same *"corruptible seed"* (1 Pet. 1.23), and therefore the inspired Word says *"seed,"* not seeds, in the same way that Christ is the one "seed" of righteousness (Gal. 3.16), which is the same seed through which all "born again" believers are renewed in God's image through the miraculous power of Christ, and endeared to Him as His children (v. 29).

It is thus that Paul calls original depravity *"our"* old man in Rom. 6.6: for all men are born with the same nature. Notwithstanding, the old man belongs to each person individually: and thus, each believer must choose by faith to receive Christ and be delivered from the old man by the Spirit's sanctifying power, regardless if other men do, or do not. Thus, in saying *"our old man is crucified with [Christ],"* Paul is speaking more particularly of all who have been sanctified by grace and faith in Christ and made free from the dominion of sin (Rom. 1.6; 1 Cor. 1.2; 2 Cor. 1.1; see also Jn. 8.36; Rom. 6.6-7, 10-14, 18-23). Therefore, though we share with all men one "old man" by natural birth, yet this same old man belongs to each one personally. Each person therefore bears his own burden of sin, and each man stands to be judged on his own record (Ezek. 18.2-4, 20). We are judged ultimately and eternally therefore not as a race but as an individual (more about this in a moment). So, while all men are born in depravity and pass on that depravity by natural generation, yet *"whosoever will"* may be delivered by the grace of Christ's atonement---the *"free gift"* of Christ, the second Adam (Rom. 5.12-19; Rev. 13.8). This explains why children born of sanctified parents are yet born in depravity. The parents cannot pass on their grace and salvation, only their depravity. For salvation is a personal choice, whereas depravity is transmitted naturally to the whole race.[15]

Now observe: Paul depicts the "old man" as a determined and stubborn spirit, desiring to live, and thus he puts up a fight "to the death" against the grace of God: for God's law *"condemns sin in the flesh"* and grace seeks to destroy sin at its source---in the heart of man. Thus, as the old man struggles to breathe and to live, the believer cries out for deliverance. This occasions a violent struggle to ensue, in which one or the other---either the new man or the old man---will finally prevail (Mt. 11.12; 12.28, 29; Lu. 11.21-26; 16.16; Eph. 6.10-18; Col. 2.11-15). One will die, the other will live. Either the flesh or the Spirit will conquer, not both; either the believer's faith and desire to serve and be like Christ will prevail, or else he will allow the power of sin to triumph over him (Jn. 8.34; Rom. 6.16; 2 Pet. 2.18-22). *"No man can serve two masters: for either he will hate the one and love the other; or else he will hold to the one and despise the other"* (Mt. 6.24). Sarah and Hagar cannot live in the same house (Gen. 21.10, 12; Gal. 4.30-31). One or the other must go! For the command of God is to be *"dead indeed unto sin, but alive to God."*

The apostle Peter's admonition and command seems to convey this same idea: *"Forasmuch then as Christ hath suffered in the flesh, arm yourselves likewise with the same mind: for he that hath*

---

[15] The arguments made by Methodist theologian John Miley in his *Systematic Theology* on native depravity and its consequences, over against the basic views of Calvinism, are insightful and worthy of consideration (see particularly Vol. I, pp. 441-533). We do not agree on every point with Miley, however: for example, his denial of a common fallen nature with Adam. He does this it seems to support his thesis that all sin is personal. While we agree that all sin is ultimately personal, we see no reason to deny a common nature with Adam to prove it: for we are finally condemned and punished not for the inherited depravity received from Adam, but for our personal acts of sin which are rooted in that depravity. And thus, accordingly, we are finally judged not for what Adam did but for what we do.

suffered in the flesh hath ceased from sin (1 Pet. 4.1). To suffer in the flesh, we take to mean primarily to struggle and fight in faith until the "old man", "the flesh" is crucified with Christ, and therewith the believer is finally *"made free from sin"*, that is, he *"has ceased from sin"*. This agrees with the apostle's further admonition and explanation in the next verse, *"That he no longer should live the rest of his time in the flesh to the lusts of men, but to the will of God"*.

Jesus must have been referring to Hagar in Jn. 8.34-36 in responding to the Jews' argument that they were Abraham's seed and, as such, were never in bondage to any man and thus stood justified before God. Jesus said, *"Whosoever committeth sin is the servant of sin. And the servant [like Hagar] abideth not in the house forever . . . ."* And this agrees with the apostle Paul's understanding and doctrine in Gal. 4.22-31.

The Lord has graciously provided a special atonement in Christ that allows no quarters for sin in the life of the child of God (Rom. 6.14; 8.5-10; Gal. 5.16-17; 2 Tim. 2:19). The "old man" therefore must be destroyed for the believer to have perfect freedom in Christ (Jn. 8.36; Rom. 6.1-2, 6, 11-18). And this is made possible in Christ's sacrificial atonement. So, whereas *"death reigned from Adam to Moses"*, now *"the gift of righteousness reigns in life by Jesus Christ."* Yes, Adam's offence brought death and suffering, but now *"much more the grace of God, and the gift of grace . . . by Jesus Christ . . . abounds unto many"* (5.14-16).

In Romans 7, Paul reflects on his former bondage to the body of sin, to empathize with others who are still in bondage, to show them the way out. He poses a question that must have come before him while he was yet in the throes of the battle with the old man, while still wrestling and struggling to be freed from his deadly grasp. He remembered crying out to God: *"O wretched that I am! Who shall deliver me from this bondage of death?"* (v. 24). Then recalled the victorious break-through and deliverance, *"I thank God through Jesus Christ our Lord"* (v. 25).

> *Amazing grace how sweet the sound*
> *That save a wretch like me!*
> *I once was lost, but now I'm found,*
> *Was blind but now I see.*

See here: if the heart of man was susceptible to deception before the fall, how much more afterward---after it was corrupted? The inspired prophet says, the heart of sinners is *"deceitful above all things, and desperately wicked: who can know it?"* (Jer. 17.9). It is paramount therefore to understand the nature of depravity and God's remedy for in Christ. Depravity is such, that even when a believer is regenerated and becomes a new creature in Christ, the inclination to sin remains; indeed, it becomes even more powerful because of the new illumination, for the "old man" feels threatened by the new life in the believer and struggles more desperately to survive and live on against the sanctifying power of the Holy Spirit (Rom. 6.12-20; 7.13-25; Gal. 4.28-31; 5.17; 2 Thess. 2.13; Heb. 10.32). Now this is true insomuch that if the new-born babe does not go on to be crucified with Christ, the "old man" will inevitably pull him down again under the dominion and corruption of sin. Paul put it like this: *"I find then a law, that, when I would do good, evil is present with me. For I delight in the law of God after the inward man: But I see another law in my members, warring against the law of my mind, and bringing me into captivity to the law of sin"* (Rom. 7.21-23). Therefore, we stand in Zion Assembly squarely in the Wesleyan tradition of faith in this regard: for Wesley and his followers proclaimed and experienced the miracle of sanctifying grace---the death of the old man and perfect freedom in Christ.

We have stated that all men are born sinners with a depraved nature. This is a point that is hotly debated by various theologians and churchmen and has separated Christians into various denominations. Many deny that men are born sinners and have inherited from Adam the nature of depravity. [16] Even some believers in holiness-Pentecostal churches deny this. We admit of course a degree of mystery here that is not fully comprehensible nor perfectly explainable; but the revelation of original sin, with its consequences, is so explicitly stated in the Scriptures (Jn. 3.36; Rom. 3.9-12, 23; 5.12-19; 1 Cor. 15.22, 45-50; Gal. 3.22; Eph. 2.2-3; 5.6; et al) and is so evident in the universal experience of man, that it cannot be reasonably contradicted. But observe; a person comes under condemnation particularly and finally because he acts out of his own depravity in willful acts of rebellion against God (Ezek. 18.2-32; Jer. 31.29-30; Jn. 3.18-20; Rom. 5.16-18; Titus 3.11; Jas. 5.12).

---

[16] In fact, it became popular in the nineteenth- and early twentieth century among certain Methodists and holiness groups to teach that infants are born Christians. The celebrated holiness scholar, William Godby, who flourished at that time believed it to be the case and thus propagated the doctrine. He wrote in *God's Revivalist* in 1910: "The wonderful redeeming grace of Christ reaches every human being the moment soul and body are united in the prenatal state and thus constitute personality. Therefore, everyone born into this world is born a Christian. At the same time, everyone is born with inbred depravity or the carnal nature dwelling in them (*God's Revivalist*, January 13, 1910). In response to Godby and others of that opinion, we say rather that this is an overreaction against Calvinism; for though all men are born in depravity, and are sinful, they are not blameworthy; for infants and small children do not become accountable and thus are not blameworthy for their "sins" until having developed a moral consciousness, thereby making them capable of sinning willfully against the commandments of God (see "Infants Born in Sin," pp. 93-100)

False Teachings about Mary and the Immaculate Conception

No one born of a woman is exempt from original sin, not even Mary, the mother of Jesus (Ps. 143.2; Eccl. 7.20; 1 Kg. 8.46; Lu. 11.13; Gal. 3.22; Rom. 3.9-10). *"There is none that doeth good, no, not one"* (Rom. 3.12), and again, *"For all have sinned, and come short of the glory of God"* (v. 23). Like her celebrated ancestor, Mary could have as well have said, *"Behold, I was shapen in iniquity, and in sin did my mother conceive me"* (Ps. 51.5).

We emphasize this point here not to diminish the honor bestowed upon Mary as the mother of our Lord, for God brought together miraculously in her womb the eternal Son of God and fitted Him with a body to establish the New Covenant in His blood (Lu.1.26-48; 1 Cor. 11.24-25). In this unique role, Mary was *"highly favored . . . among [not above] women"* and *"found favor with God"* (Lu. 1.28-35). But the Roman Catholic doctrine of the Immaculate Conception---that Mary was born "free from all stain of original sin"[17]---seriously violates the plain revelation of the Holy Scriptures in favor of an inordinate exaltation of Mary based on vain tradition and time-honored errors.

The native depravity of Mary may be seen further in this: after she gave birth to Jesus, she was considered unclean and required to observe the act of purification (Lu. 2.22); then after thirty-three days, according to traditional Jewish practice, a sin offering would have been made for her cleansing (Lev. 12.4-6). There are also several instances in which Jesus relegated Mary to a place in

---

[17] Richard P. McBrien, gen ed. *The HarperCollins Encyclopedia of Catholicism* (New York: HarperCollins Publishers, 1995), pp 655-656.

common with all men (Mt. 12.46-50; Lu. 8.21; 11.27; Jn. 2.4; 12.19.26-27).

Clearly, Christ is the only person who has ever been conceived without sin (1 Cor. 5.21; Heb. 4.15; 7.26; 1 Pet. 2.22; 1 Jn. 3.5); and this was made possible only by a special and miraculous operation of the Holy Spirit, not because of Mary's virginity, nor of any inherent virtue in Mary, nor of any virtue in the mother of Mary (Lu. 1.30-35; Heb. 4.15; 9.14; 1 Pet. 1.19; 2.22).

Jesus is the *"firstborn of every creature"* and the *"firstborn from the dead"* (Col. 1.15-18; Rev.1.5-8), that is, He is the beginning of a new [or renewed] human race (1 Pet. 2.5-9), a race restored by grace through faith (Eph. 2.5, 8), and destined to be perfected through love in Christ's image (Rom. 8.29; Col. 3.10); whereas, the doctrine of the Immaculate Conception logically, either wittingly or unwittingly, makes Mary the first born of a new race. This is heresy! Moreover, several other unfounded speculations follow in the train of this primary error regarding Mary: to wit, "perpetual virginity," "Mother of God," mediatorial intercessions for the church and sinners, and in general an exalted veneration of her person and function. It is thus purported by the Roman Church that she was "born in grace not in sin," and that "in her very being . . . the grip of evil is broken." If that be the case, Mary would not have needed a Savior. Again, the idea is unthinkable and heretical.

The Council of Trent in 1545-1563, to avoid the internal controversies in the Roman Church over Mary and original sin, particularly the objections raised by such influential men as Anselm (d. 1109), Bernard (d. 1153), Bonaventure (d. 1174), and Aquinas (d. 1274), avoided the subject of original sin relative to Mary, and decreed rather that she was "free from all sins from the moment of her existence and throughout her entire life." This of course was simply a crafty way of saying the same thing. Overall, the fictitious and irreverent portrait of Mary by the Roman Catholic Church has no resemblance to the mother of Jesus in the Bible. But let us here return to our primary thesis.

Common Depravity versus
Personal Accountability

We have emphasized that our inherited depravity is sinful, yet men are not finally condemned for it unless they reject God's remedy for it in Christ and thereby choose to make it their own. For men are blamed and finally condemned only for the sinful choices they make after becoming morally responsible persons, that is, after a moral consciousness has developed within them as human beings. This state or condition of moral consciousness and responsibility has been called the "age of accountability". It is then that men choose to repent and accept the grace of Christ's atonement and cleansing power, or otherwise to do *"despite the grace of Christ"* and so prove themselves more effectually to be sinners (Jn. 1.11-12; 3.16, 36; Acts 16.30-31; Rom. 8.5-9; Eph. 2.2-3; Col. 3.6-7).

Sin thus exists in two forms: primarily, in the very being of man, in his depraved nature (Rom. 6.6; Eph. 2.3), and secondarily, in personal acts of transgression (Eph. 2.1; Col. 2.13). The former is called "original sin," and is the source of all acts of transgression and disobedience, that is, men commit acts of sin under the powerful influence of their depraved moral nature, freely choosing to yield to the inclination of inborn lusts and desires. Jesus said all men are born in darkness and are lost (Lu. 19.10; Jn. 12.46; see also Ps. 51.5; 53.2-3; 58.3) and their hearts are evil (Mt. 15.19; Lu. 11.13); and thus, they need to be born again and sanctified (Jn. 3.3-

8; 17.17-19). See Paul's thought in Rom. 1.21; Col. 1.13, and Peter's conclusion in 1 Pet. 1.23.

Because of inherited depravity, men are *"in sin conceived"*, *"shapen in iniquity"* and *"estranged from the womb"* (Ps. 51.5; 58.3). They are born thus with the inclination to sin and are by *"nature the children of wrath"* (Eph. 2.2-3): for God foreseeing their unwillingness to repent, accordingly foreordained their judgment. Now observe, acknowledgement that one is in the grip of the "old man" is the *first step* toward being delivered; believing that Christ has the power to break his grip is the *second step*; crying out in faith to be delivered is the *third step*.

Let it be a settled point, however, that God's judgment is not against the nature of depravity *per se,* as if our inherited depravity in and of itself sins and thus incurs God's wrath; rather God judges an individual finally for his personal acts of disobedience which have their source in that depravity (Deut. 24.16; 2 Kg. 14.6; Jer. 31.29-30; Ezek. 18.4-20; Rom. 2.5-10; Gal 6.5-8). Thus, when we become conscious of the depravity within us, we become responsible for it---we make it our own! We then become responsible to seek God's remedy for it in Christ, namely, that glorious second work of grace---sanctification!

In the final analysis sin is therefore judged on a personal basis. In other words, there is no blameworthy sin where there is no morally responsible person to commit it. Thus, no man is finally condemned and damned because of inherited depravity or original sin, but rather for the acts committed that arise from the Adamic nature. Again, as already noticed, this accounts for the salvation of infants and small children; for though they are born with depravity, they are not held accountable for it (see "Infants Born in Sin", pp. 93-100).

Observe; Adam sinned against the direct and explicit commandment of God in Eden (Gen. 2.16-17; 3.1-7; 1 Tim. 2.13-

14), but men thereafter sinned not as Adam had done, but rather by defying and disobeying the natural laws that God had set in motion, and the moral law that He had engraved in man's consciousness (Rom. 1.20; 2.1, 14-15); Thus, Paul says, *"Nevertheless death reigned . . . even over those who had not sinned according to the likeness of the transgression of Adam"* (5.14). Then, after the written law was established through Moses, men sinned more boldly and blatantly against explicit commandments. In any case, it was the act of personal and willful disobedience that brought the righteous judgment of God. We see this in Cain (in the sin of murder) and thereafter in Lamech (in the sins of adultery and killing) and in all those who followed, until the *"wickedness of man was great in the earth."* The Lord judged all according to their deeds, destroying the world with the great flood, saving only Noah and his family (Gen. 6.1-8; 7.1, 11-23). Even in the oft quoted Pauline passage in Eph. 2.3 that Calvinists are fond of quoting to prove their argument of imputed guilt and punishment upon all men because of Adam's first sin, a careful examination of the passage rather proves the opposite: that is, Adam's descendants are rather blamed for their own sinful actions, not their common depravity (vv. 2-5).

John Wesley versus John Calvin

Why and how was Noah saved nearly 2500 years before Christ was born? He *"found grace in the eyes of the Lord"* (Gen. 6.8), and *"was a just man and perfect in his generations"* (v. 9); and, like his great-grandfather Enoch before him, he *"walked with God"* (5.24). But how was this possible in man's fallen state? According to Wesley over against the opinions of Calvin, it was because the Lord continued to commune with man, with a gracious view for his salvation, and man retained, even in his fallen state, the ability to choose his own destiny. Wesley saw in this gracious operation of God a pre-condition of the atonement. He called it "preventing grace".[18] Accordingly, God having foreseen man's fall, foreordained that His Son should be *"slain from the foundation of the world"* to atone for man's disobedience and rebellion, and thus provided the means for redemption and reconciliation in the *covenant of mercy* (Rev. 13.8; 17.8; cf. also Rom. 8.29-30; Eph. 1.4-9; 2.1-8; 2 Tim. 1.9-10). Else God's wrath would have severely judged and punished man in his sin in the beginning in Eden and destroyed him from off the face of the earth. Christ is therefore our *"propitiation"* (Rom. 3.25; Heb. 2.17-18; 1 Jn. 2.2; 4.10); that is, the sacrifice of Christ *"from the foundation of the world"* turned away God's vehement wrath, and prompted Him rather to graciously *"[give] light to every man coming into the world"* (Jn. 1.9; also Rom. 8.29-30; 12.3; 2 Tim. 1.9-10; Titus 2.11), and, again contrary to Calvin and his followers, to grant salvation to all who believe and accept the atoning sacrifice of God's Son (Rom. 5.11; Eph. 2.1-8; Titus 2.11). Indeed, *"where sin abounded, grace did much more abound . . . so might grace reign through righteousness unto eternal life by Jesus Christ our Lord"* (Rom. 5.20-21).

> *Grace, grace, God's grace,*
> *Grace that will pardon and cleanse within;*
> *Grace, grace, God's grace,*
> *Grace that is greater than all our sin!*

---

[18] John Wesley, *The Works of John Wesley,* 15 Vols. (Grand Rapids: Baker Book House: reprint 1984 of 1872 edition): VI, pp. 215-252. See also John Wesley, *New Testament: Translation and Notes in Modern English*, 2 Vols., (Nicholasville, KY: Schmul Publishing Co., 2012), II, pp. 337-339. The idea of "prevenient grace" was not original with Wesley; it was taught by Roman Catholics for centuries and defined in the Council of Trent in 1545-63, and thereafter carried over into the Church of England in the sixteenth century.

Significantly, A. H. Strong, an early twentieth century scholar and Calvinist, admitted that Calvin and his followers in the first centuries of the Great Reformation did not take into account what Wesley and his followers brought to light in the eighteenth- and nineteenth centuries: namely, "that there was a total redemption, over against man's total depravity," provided by the grace of *the Lamb slain from the foundation of the world*" even while Adam was yet in the very motion of falling. Indeed, original grace antedated original sin! Says the learned theologian,

"Our fathers believed in total depravity, and we agree with them that man naturally is devoid of love to God and that every faculty is weakened, disordered, and corrupted by the selfish bent of his will. They held to original sin. The selfish bent of man's will can be traced back to the apostacy of our first parents; and, on account of that departure of the race from God, all men are by nature children of wrath. And all this is true, if it is regarded as a statement of the facts, apart from their relation to Christ. But our fathers did not see, as we do, that man's relation to Christ antedated the Fall and constituted an underlying and modifying condition of man's life. Humanity was naturally in Christ, in whom all things were created and in whom they all consist. Even man's sin did not prevent Christ from still working in him to counteract the evil and to suggest the good. There was an internal, as well as an external, preparation for man's redemption. In this sense of a divine principle in man striving against the selfish and godless will, there was a total redemption, over against man's total depravity; and an original grace, that was even more powerful than original sin.

"We have become conscious that total depravity alone is not a sufficient or proper expression of the truth; and the phrase has been outgrown. It has been felt that the old view of sin did not take account of the generous and noble aspirations, the unselfish efforts, the strivings after God, of even unregenerate men. For this reason, there has been less preaching about sin, and less conviction as to its guilt and condemnation. The good impulses of men outside the Christian pale have been often credited to human nature, when they should have been credited to the indwelling Spirit of Christ. I make no doubt that one of our radical weaknesses at this present time is our more superficial view of sin. Without some sense of sin's guilt and condemnation, we cannot feel our need of redemption. John the Baptist must go before Christ; the law must prepare the way for the gospel.

"My belief is that the new apprehension of Christ's relation to the race will enable us to declare, as never before, the lost condition of the sinner; while at the same time we show him that Christ is with him and in him to save. This presence in every man of a power not his own that works for righteousness is a very different doctrine from that 'divinity of man' which is so often preached. The divinity is not the divinity of man, but the divinity of Christ. And the power that works for righteousness is not the power of man, but the power of Christ. It is a power whose warning, inviting, persuading influence renders only more marked and dreadful the evil will which hampers and resists it. Depravity is all the worse, when we recognize in it the constant antagonist of an ever-present, all-holy, and all-loving Redeemer."[19]

This is quite an admission by the learned Calvinist professor, which he made in a sermon delivered in Cleveland, Ohio in May 1904 while serving as president and professor of biblical theology at Rochester Theological Seminary in New York. Clearly his sentiments in this sermon agree more with Wesley than Calvin. While holding firm to total depravity and inherited guilt with condemnation and eternal punishment, he had become enlightened to the truth that God's grace and mercy in Christ through His atonement antedated the fall of man and its consequences: and thus that "original grace . . . was even more powerful than original sin."

Notwithstanding, we cannot agree with the learned professor's view of "the indwelling of the Spirit of Christ" in sinners to bring them under the impact of conviction toward repentance. In this respect, Strong sounds more like a Quaker than a Calvinist or a Wesleyan: for Quakers were guilty of that very error: mistaking the "inner light" or voice of conscience for the Holy Spirit. While the Holy Spirit is omnipresent and thus, in some sense may be said to work within unregenerate men, particularly within their consciences (Jn. 1.9); yet it is clear in the Scriptures that the Spirit speaks and works efficiently from without the sinner convicting his spirit, agitating his conscience, calling him to repentance, striving with him, and "drawing" him to God (Gen. 6.3; Jn. 6.44; 12.32; Acts 9.1-18). The phrase *"indwelling of the Spirit"* [or *"abiding in Christ"*] is rather used in the context of regenerate believers, not unregenerate men (Rom. 8.9-11; 1 Cor. 3.16; 6.19; 2 Cor. 6.16; Gal. 4.6; Phil. 1.19; see also Jn. 14.23; et al).

---

[19] Strong, *Systematic Theology*, pp. 551-552.

In any case, it was thus that the *"God of all grace"* gave to man even in his fallen state the promise of and accessibility to the Gospel of mercy (Gen. 3.15; Eph. 1.4-9; 2.1-5). He has called and anointed preachers to preach the Gospel (2 Pet. 2.5; Jude 14-16); and His Spirit strives with man to repent and assures all men of His blessings if they will heed to His gracious call (Rom. 10.13; Titus 2.4; 2 Pet. 3.9; Rev. 22.17). The foreordained sacrifice and sufferings of Christ turned away the anger and wrath of God, making propitiation for all who believe, reconciling them in love and mercy (Rom. 3.5; 2 Cor. 5.18; 1 Jn. 2.2; 4.10).

The Spirit's cry, *"Save yourselves from this generation"* (Acts 2.40), was thus heard even in Adam's day, and has echoed down the corridors of time to every generation since (1 Pet. 3.18-20). Noah thus could have been numbered with the multitudes in whom *"every imagination of the thoughts of [their hearts were] only evil continually"* (Gen. 6.5), but he rather *"found grace in the eyes of the Lord"* and chose the *"narrow way"* of a holy life over against the *"broad way"* of destruction (Mt. 7.13-14, 21-26).

> *O victory in Jesus, my Savior, forever,*
> *He sought me and bo't me with His redeeming blood;*
> *He loved me ere I knew Him, and all my love is due Him,*
> *He plunged me to victory, be-neath the cleansing flood.*

We have seen that, notwithstanding that all men are born with depravity, in the final analysis they commit sin not by a necessity of their fallen nature but by their own choice. In doing so they reject *"the grace of God that [brings] salvation [and that has] appeared to all men"* (Titus 2.11), and rather *will* to sin, being *"drawn away"* by their own lusts into disobedience (Jas. 1.14-15; 4.2-3; Eph. 2.2-3). Thus, the blameworthy sinner consciously, personally, and deliberately chooses to disobey God (Jn. 9.41;

Rom. 1.20-23, 32; 2.14-18; Heb. 10.26; 2 Pet. 3.5; Jas. 4.17). Even many Calvinists in the last century have admitted that Scriptural evidence and reason have forced them to admit to this truth, that for one to be blameworthy and eternally condemned and punished it must be through a conscious act of free will. The esteemed Professor Strong, whom we quoted earlier, admitted finally after God had opened his eyes that "no human being is finally condemned solely on account of original sin; but that all who, like infants, do not commit personal transgressions, are saved through the application of Christ's atonement; that our responsibility for inborn evil dispositions, or for the depravity common to the race, can be maintained only upon the ground that this depravity was caused by an original and conscious act of the will".[20]

Still, to remain in the camp of the Calvinists, the professor then argues for the typical federal headship of Adam and blames all men for acting together with Adam in committing the original sin in Eden. Again, we find this theological position untenable and nonsensical. For in seeking redemption and reconciliation with God we repent and ask forgiveness for the actual sins we have committed, not for the depraved nature we inherited. We first ask as a sinner for pardon for our transgressions, not for Adam's; then as a born-again believer we seek to be delivered from and cleansed of the "sin nature" within us. We are first justified, then sanctified wholly: and each of these works of grace is instantaneous and definite; further, both experiences---justification and sanctification---happen in an hour of crisis. In justification/regeneration *the sinner* is brought to a critical moment in which he cries out for peace and reconciliation with God (Rom. 5.1); in sanctification, *the believer* cries out for deliverance from

---

[20] Strong, *Systematic Theology*, p. 596.

the "old man", and to be restored wholly in the divine image of Christ (6.1-6; 7.24-25; 1 Thess. 5.23).

It may be seen, then, that we disagree in several significant points with many of the basic teachings of Augustine, Martin Luther, John Calvin, and other celebrated leaders and theologians in Christian history who have had a tremendous impact on the thinking and development of modern-day Christianity.[21] Calvin, following in the steps of Augustine and Luther, for example, went so far to assert that all men are so depraved by their fallen nature that they lack the ability of a free moral agency to repent and be reconciled to God by grace and faith; and, therefore, accordingly, all depends on God's sovereign will and decree. Accordingly, the Almighty elects some to salvation and consigns others to eternal damnation. Some are therefore pulled to salvation by an "irresistible grace," while others are pulled into darkness and damnation by an irresistible evil. Thus the "elect" are unconditionally saved, even against their own wills. In Calvin's view, the image of God was so destroyed by the fall of man, that man was no longer man, that is, he lacked a free moral agency; indeed, in this sense, he inherited a nature at birth that relegated him to a beast or an idiot, a mind so vitiated that God could no longer reason with him. Thus, man in general was rendered incapable of hearing the Gospel and repenting. In a word, God determined, wholly on His own, to save some, and to destroy others.[22]

---

[21] An insightful treatment of the superiority of the Arminian-Wesleyan perspective of fallen man and redemption over against the Calvinistic view is Richard S. Taylor, *A Right Conception of Sin* (Nicholasville, KY: Schmul Publishing Company, 2002).

[22] The term used by Luther to support his argument was *monergism* [over against *synergism*], signifying that salvation is wholly the work of God, even to the absolute exclusion of man's co-operation in the process of justification. He

The old Calvinistic view of the Gospel clearly contradicts the Word of God, reason, and human experience. The Scriptures reveal plainly that, though man fell morally and spiritually in Eden, yet he retained the ability to reason with God and, as a free moral agent, remained capable of responding to the call of God to be saved or to reject God and be damned (Gen. 9.6; Is. 1.18; 43.25-26; Mic. 6.2; Mk. 1.14; Jn. 3.1-36). Moreover, Calvin taught that God predetermined the fall of man to make election and reprobation possible, and He did this for His own glory. Imagine that! Accordingly, God himself is responsible for man's fall, and consequently the author of sin![23]

It was because Calvin's theology was flawed at its very foundation that he was led to construct the warped doctrines of strict predestination (pre-necessitation), limited atonement (Jesus died only for those whom God had eternally decreed to be saved), and perseverance or eternal security---*once in grace always in grace!* Moreover, some others, under the influence of Calvin's theology, have been led to develop certain lawless ("antinomian") doctrines and, ironically, the heresy of universalism, the latter of which purports that in the end all men will be saved. Witness the

---

based his extreme thinking in this regard on his belief that man lost his freewill in the fall. [Note his treatise on "The Bondage of the Will"]. Luther pressed this point until he made a complete *reduction ad absurdum* of his whole hypothesis. Even his chief theologian, Philip Melanchthon, finally found this position untenable. But Calvin took the view to the extreme in developing his system of absolute determinism. Luther's views on the fall of man, freewill and salvation were influenced by Manichaeism via the writings of Augustine, and both Augustine and Luther in turn influenced Calvin.

[23] John Calvin, *Institutes of the Christian Religion* (Grand Rapids: Eerdmans Publishing Company, 1983, reprint). Celebrated historian Will Durant is perhaps right in stating that Calvin's *Institutes* was "One of the Ten books that shook the world." The *Institutes* are Calvin's *magnum opus*, in which his entire theology is set forth. Relative to our study in this book on sin, his erroneous thinking regarding the fall of man, the results of the fall, and man's redemption are especially set forth in Book II, pp. 209-298 of his *Institutes*.

work of the Swiss Reformed theologian Karl Barth (1886-1968), whose celebrated ideas in the last century were merely a revamping of several of the essential points of Calvin's old system. It is for these reasons we feel obligated to expose Calvin's erroneous teachings: for they distort grace and encourage lawlessness; for if the destiny of all men has been predetermined solely by God's sovereign decree, even before He created the world, why cry out for deliverance from sin and seek for holiness?

We may be thankful that John Wesley, following in the tradition of the radical reformers, advanced in the light of the prophetic Word and restored Gospel grace and the *covenant of mercy*: namely, the power of God that calls men to repentance without respect to persons and effectively purges "all sin" through His sanctifying power in all who respond willingly in faith, translating them into *"the kingdom of [God's] dear Son"* (Col. 1.13; 2 Pet. 3.9).

Sin and Guilt

Contrary to the followers of Calvin, we do not hold to the doctrine that the guilt of Adam's transgression in the Garden was transmitted to all men; at least not in the sense that Adam is considered the representative or federal head of all men, and therefore that all men committed that first act of disobedience with him, and thus are personally responsible and eternally punishable for that act of defiance and disobedience. This old theory, propagated by celebrated Calvinistic theologians such as Jonathan Edwards, Charles Hodge and other Princeton divines, is rooted in Augustinian anthropology, which in turn had been influenced by

Manichaeism[24]. While it is true that Adam's transgression was "passed on" to his posterity, and thus all men inherit from him by natural generation a depraved nature; yet it is not true that all men somehow committed that first sin with him, nor that all men are guilty and condemned and deserve eternal punishment for the sin that Adam committed in Eden. For the apostle Paul seems to be emphatic in stressing that *"by one man sin entered into the world"* (Rom. 5.12), not by all men. Again, he repeatedly emphasizes that *"if through the offence of one many be dead"*, and *"by one man's offence death resigned"*, and *"by the offence of one judgment came"*, and yet again *"by one man's disobedience many were made sinners"* (vv. 15-19)

An extreme, if not absurd, interpretation of Augustine's anthropology is rooted in philosophical realism, represented in the works of William G. T. Shedd. Like most Calvinists, it purports the idea of the generic unity of man, generic transgression, and generic condemnation with guilt and eternal punishment. Yet this view is more extreme, holding that *mankind* necessarily existed before men were created, and *nature* existed before the individuals who were produced out of it.[25] This is nothing short of old paganism and a reassertion of Middle Ages scholastic *realism*---

---

[24] Augustine had been a Manichean for nine years before his conversion in A.D. 386. In his *Confessions* he candidly describes his conversion and deliverance from sin and Manichaeism; yet it seems plain that he continued unwittingly to be influenced by Manichean philosophy from which he had drunk so deeply as a young man. Particularly he retained Mani's doctrine that unregenerate men since the fall in Eden lacked freewill and therefore could not perform any good work. Further, Mani taught that sexuality wars against the soul and pulls it downward toward sin. These ideas we see so plainly in Augustine's views on original sin and its transmission through concupiscence, and also his affinity with the ideal of asceticism. Calvin and his followers in turn beginning in the sixteenth century pressed Augustine's views into full-blown Calvinism.

[25] William G. T. Shedd, *Dogmatic Theology*, 3 Vols. (Nashville: Thomas Nelson Publishers, 1980, reprint), II, pp. 14-16, 38, 45.

the philosophical argument that universals have objective reality, and that material objects exist in themselves apart from the mind's consciousness of them. Accordingly, individuals have no separate being in themselves, but rather are mere modes and manifestations of the preexistent *generic nature*. In other words, though we may have been born three thousand years after Adam, yet we were in his loins, and thus committed the first sin with him. The whole race of man voluntarily committed the apostatizing act in Adam. This is pure speculation and, we believe, sheer nonsense. It is pantheism wrapped in the pretense of Christian doctrine, and smacks also of Platonism on one hand and materialism on the other.

A somewhat modified view of this realism admits that the individual has the essence of existence in himself, yet that essence also previously existed in the generic nature before the individuals received their separate existence.[26] In either case, whether before the individualization of Adam's posterity or afterward, the total being of all generations existed in the preexistent generic nature. Thus, accordingly, Adam contained within him the essence of all future generations, so that what he did, they did, and thus they were just as guilty as he for the act that he committed in Eden.[27]

The more widely accepted Augustinian-Calvinistic view was championed by the influential Charles Hodge of the "Princeton School" in the nineteenth century. This view was afterward perpetuated by the celebrated Louis Berkhof in the twentieth century, especially through his influential *Systematic Theology* published in 1949.[28] It views Adam not only as the natural head of

---

[26] Charles Hodge, *Systematic Theology*, 3 Vols. (Grand Rapids, MI: Wm. B. Eerdmans, 1979), II, pp. 220-227.

[27] Miley, *Systematic Theology*, I, pp. 474-476.

[28] Louis Berkhof, *Systematic Theology* (Grand Rapids, MI: Wm. B. Eerdmans Publishing Co., 1949), pp. 211-264.

the whole race of man, but also the federal head on the judicial ground of the covenant of works. Accordingly, as the federal head of the covenant, what Adam was and did implicated his posterity, and was passed on to his descendants. The sin that he committed with its penalties, including eternal death and damnation, was *imputed* to his posterity---to every man---because he was ordained the federal head of the race. In this view, though Adam's descendants did not commit with him that first act of disobedience in Eden, the act of Adam was yet imputed to them. Thus, all that he did was reckoned to the account of his descendants, including its penalties---guilt of the first sin, loss of original righteousness, corruption of the whole nature, and suffering and punishment including spiritual, temporal, and eternal death.[29]

Arminian-Wesleyan Perspective

The ministers and members of Zion Assembly stand in the tradition of the Arminian-Wesleyan tradition of the faith regarding the nature of sin, its transmission, and remedy, particularly as it was more finely thought-through and defined by Wesleyan scholars beginning in the nineteenth century. As such, we admit that men are alienated from God and act out of a common depravity passed on to us because of Adam's sin and our racial relationship with him; and further we admit that this depraved nature is the basis for all sin, and that the depraved nature is itself sinful. The sinfulness of depravity is self-evident in human experience, to which all fair-minded men will admit: for all are born with an inclination to lust for evil things, to harden their

---

[29] Charles Hodge, *Systematic Theology* [1 Vol., abridged edition], (Grand Rapids: Baker Book House, 1988), pp. 289-296.

hearts, and to manifest on occasion ill affections, feelings, and emotions. It is true that many deny original sin, and even deny the reality of sin itself, yet almost all men admit that they have a propensity to act contrary to the right and good; and, thus, in this way admit to the depraved nature.

Still, though we agree with the Augustinian-Calvinistic doctrine of total depravity inherited by all men because of the fall of Adam, we reject the assertion that the personal sin of Adam with its guilt and eternal punishment has been imputed to all men in all generations. To concede some points to Calvinism does not require that we admit to the whole system. We agree that all morally-responsible men sense a certain guilt that arises from one's separation and alienation from God, and that they are born with a bent toward evil rooted in native depravity; and that this state of being is *"passed upon"* [or "spread"] to all men through Adam. In this sense, it may be said that Adam's fall and certain aspects of its consequences were reckoned upon or imputed to all men. But we reject that one person's guilt with eternal consequences can be transmitted and imputed with blame to another person; for this would necessarily include infants and small children, and thus we would be thrown back to the Augustinianism of the fourth century and the doctrine of the apostate church of the Dark Ages, which led to infant baptisms and many other corresponding errors and corruptions. Wesleyan himself, though at times seeming to agree with Calvinists on many of the essential points of the Calvinistic system yet stated unequivocally that "[God] will punish no man for doing anything which he could possibly avoid; neither for omitting anything which he could possibly do. Every punishment supposes the offender might have avoided the offense for which he is punished: Otherwise to punish him would be palpably unjust, and inconsistent with the character of God our Governor".[30]

Our case thus may be stated in the following manner: when we become conscious of our alienation or estrangement from God and cognizant of God's law, that is, having arrived at the "age of accountability" (more about this in a moment), we will feel a sense of guilt for our depraved state of being and propensity toward sin; for we then make our inherited depravity our own and consequently become personally accountable for it. Moreover, this becomes more especially the case if we continue to resist the Holy Spirit's call to repentance and reconciliation with God through the mercy and gracious means He provided for us in Christ---to wit, the unspeakable love and sacrifice of the Father in giving His only-begotten Son, and the wonder and love of the Son in enduring the contradiction of sinners and being willing to lay down His life to redeem and sanctify any and all without respect to persons. For, when our moral consciousness has fully developed and we become aware of God's law and our alienation from God, and yet continue to resist His call and means for salvation we become deserving of condemnation and eternal punishment. And, contrary to the Calvinistic doctrine of perseverance, this is all the more true in cases of backsliding and apostasy: Recall the words of the inspired writer of Hebrews: *"He that despised Moses' law died without mercy under two or three witnesses: Of how much sorer punishment suppose ye, shall he be thought worthy, who hath trodden underfoot the Son of God, and **hath counted the blood of the covenant, wherein he was sanctified and unholy thing, and hath done despite the Spirit of grace"*** (Heb. 10.28-29). And again,

---

[30] John Wesley, *Calvinism Calmly Considered* (Nicholasville, KY: Schmul Publishing Co., 2001), p. 14.

for *"they crucify to themselves the Son of God afresh and put him to an open shame"* (6.6).

We admit further that in some mysterious way all morally conscious beings may share a deep psychological guilt with the whole family of fallen man. For, besides the reasons stated above regarding the evil bent in our nature, we see in the biblical narratives a kind of guilt by familial relation or corporate identity, and a liability connected with this identity (e.g., Josh. 7.10-26; Is. 6.5; Jer. 3.25; 7.19-20; 14.20; Neh. 1.6; Ezra 9.6; et al.). We do not deny therefore a certain universal guilt in the whole race of man: a kind of guilt by association, which may be the root cause of the psychological problems that many deal with as adults, including a sense of alienation from God and identity with the errors and sins common to the whole fallen race.

> *There is a fountain filled with blood*
> *Drawn from Immanuel's veins;*
> *And sinners, plunged beneath that flood,*
> *Lose all their guilty stains*

We see also that the Lord reckoned uncleanness and guilt in some sense even to those who were unconscious of their sin (Lev. 4.1-3, 13-21; 5.2-3, 17), sins which were removed, however, by the atonement offered up by the priests, typifying the atonement of Christ who is our true guilt offering (Is. 53.10). We hold therefore that all men inherit the common judgment and punishment occasioned by the fall of Adam, including physical death and suffering, yet not the guilt of Adam's personal transgression, nor eternal punishment because of it. Rather we incur guilt and eternal punishment because of our own sins, including our native depravity once we become self-conscious of our sinful nature and alienation from God, and yet reject God's remedy for our depraved state of being through the sanctifying grace of Christ and the quickening power of the Holy Spirit.

It is precisely at this point that Calvinism goes far astray from the teachings of Scripture, presuming and multiplying speculations in a most startling manner; incorporating, in part or whole, several ancient pagan and philosophical ideas tainted with Gnosticism, Platonism, Pantheism, and Universalism. The idea that all men, even before they are born, somehow participate and are implicated in Adam's personal sin and thus share in his guilt for the crime he committed is a product of fiction, not biblical revelation. Where does one go at that point with such a doctrine? It is no less absurd to say that Solomon participated in his father's adultery and murder, and equally in his repentance and redemption. Or to hold that all men are implicated in every other man's sin.

Notwithstanding these irreconcilable ideas, we acknowledge that all men suffer from the consequences of Adam's transgression in Eden, and that human depravity is dark and universal. We readily endeavor therefore to press this sobering truth upon men's minds; for only by acknowledging this deep sinful condition common to all men---original sin---will believers press to find solutions for many of the dark problems that haunt and torment men's minds and souls. We hasten to add, however, that the most efficient solution is God's sanctifying power---the crucifixion of the old man with his deeds (Rom. 6.6-7; Gal. 5.24; 6.14). Thus, Paul says, *"I am crucified with Christ: nevertheless I live; yet not I, but Christ liveth in me: and the life which I now live in the flesh I live by the faith of the Son of God . . ."* (Gal. 2.20); and again, *"But God forbid that I should glory, save in the cross of our Lord Jesus Christ, by whom the world is crucified unto me, and I unto the world"* (6.14). We also agree with professor Strong's argument for the need of a right view of sin: "I make no doubt that one of our radical weaknesses at this present time is our superficial view of sin. Without some sense of guilt and condemnation, we cannot feel our need of redemption."[31]

Whatever else may be hidden in God about sin and guilt, and how these may be transmitted in the race from generation to generation---genetically, spiritually, or otherwise---we see no profit in speculating and caviling over. For there are subtle theological and psychological mysteries which may never be fully understood on this side of glory. Some things are simply too high and too deep for us. We know, for example, that Cain inherited the nature of depravity from his father, yet he was not judged and punished for his father's depravity and transgression but for his own (Gen. 4.1-16). His depravity inclined him to murder his brother, but he chose as a free moral agent to commit that hideous crime: and it was this act that condemned him. Likewise, Seth was procreated in his father's *own likeness, in his own image"* (5.3): but he stood as an independent being, responsible and accountable for his own actions. It is so with every sinner and every sin.

More importantly, contrary to Calvin's doctrine, we do not believe that God left man in a state of total depravity without recourse to His great grace and mercy; nor that his personality was so corrupted that he was unable to freely respond to God's grace; rather, consistent with the Arminian-Wesleyan tradition of faith, we believe the universal atonement of Christ gave man the ability to respond freely to the Gospel and, at the same time, made him morally responsible for his actions.

As we have seen, Wesley believed in racial sin and guilt, but he believed in "preventing grace", by which he meant that Christ's redemptive work and the universal operation of the Holy Spirit anticipated the fall, and graciously absolved man of any guilt connected with Adam's personal sin; and, further, that this grace

---

[31] Strong, *Systematic Theology*, p. 552.

enabled men through faith to cooperate with God in His work of salvation. Whether or not Wesley was on target perfectly in all points in this regard may be argued, but his basic premise (in contradiction of Calvinism) has plenty of support in the Scriptures (Jn. 17.22; Rom. 5.15; 8.27-33; 2 Cor. 5.19, 21; Eph. 1.4-7, 11; Col. 1.15-17; 1 Pet.1.2, 18-20, 24; Rev. 13.8; 17.8; Ps. 32.2). We admit of course that there remains a degree of mystery here that cannot be fully explained, and which no human theory can fully solve. Nevertheless, the Scriptures plainly come down on the side of personal accountability based on man's freedom, and a universal redemption based on the timeless and all-pervasive grace of Christ. Thus, though a man may be totally depraved, he is not totally devoid of grace, even in sin. Wesley maintained, in fact, that a man commits sin not because he has not grace, but because he does, and yet goes his way contrary to that grace, that is, he does *"despite unto the Spirit of grace"* (Heb. 10.29). We stand therefore with Arminius and Wesley over against the Augustinian-Calvinistic tradition of faith on the one hand, the latter of which is shared by many of our friends in the Presbyterian, Lutheran, and Baptist traditions; and over against the Pelagian tradition on the other, which denies original sin: a doctrine shared by our friends in the Disciples of Christ, Churches of Christ, Quakers, Universalists, and a few other fringe groups appearing on the scene beginning in the twentieth century.

The contribution of Wesley was this: he offered a gracious alternative to Rome, Pelagius, Luther, and Calvin. He admitted original sin and its punitive consequences but offered a more benevolent and merciful view of grace than Augustine, Luther, and Calvin; one which accords, in his own words, with "the whole tenor of Scripture." His interpretation of salvation included profound responsibilities on man's part, but great mercy on God's part in His willingness to reach out to deliver all men everywhere to the uttermost. Thus, though we are born with a totally depraved nature (contrary to Pelagius' doctrine), we are judged finally not for what Adam did (contrary to Augustine and Calvin), but for what we are and what we do personally in the light of Christ's atonement and universal grace which God honored *"before the foundation of the world"*.

Thus, though man is born totally depraved he is not born totally abandoned. True, the fall of Adam and its consequences cast a dark shadow over man and left him in a morally corruptible state of being. But God did not leave him in that state without a way out: for the grace of the second Adam was immediately present to redeem and cleanse and remove the sentence of death, and to forgive and heal the wound of sin caused by the first Adam (Rom. 5.12-19; 12.3; 1 Cor. 15.21-22, 45-49; Eph. 2.2-8; Titus 2.11-15).

> *Once like a bird in prison I dwelt,*
> *No freedom from my sorrow I felt;*
> *But Jesus came and listened to me*
> *And glory to God, He set me free.*

In the light of the glorious promises of the Gospel, there is not an atom of truth in the Calvinistic scheme of eternal decrees--- "double predestination" (that God ordained some men to be saved and others eternally damned), "limited atonement" (that Jesus died only for those whom God ordained and knew would be saved), and "perseverance" (that a man who is chosen to be saved by God's eternal and sovereign decree "will never finally fall away").

We admit, of course, that we are constituted one race in Adam; yet all humans together are not one person. Therefore, while we have a unity of nature in Adam, we have not a unity of persons. Each of us is constituted a unique person and thus each of us stands uniquely accountable to God for our actions (Prov. 9.12; Ezek.

18.19-29; Rom. 14.12; Gal. 6.5; Jas. 4.17; 1 Pet. 4.5). David thus says, *"I was conceived in iniquity"* and *"I have sinned"*. Jesus says, *"To him that overcometh will I grant to sit with me in my throne"*, and again, *"if any man hear my voice, and open the door, I will come in to him, and will sup with him, and he with me"*. So, each of us is judged on our own record (cf. Mt. 12.35-37; Rom. 14.12; Jas. 4.17). The question asked by the Philippian jailor has both a personal and universal application, *"What must I do to be saved?"* And Jesus' invitation is also personal and universal: *"Whosoever will, let him come, and take the water of life freely."*

We disagree also with many Calvinists in the following point: a man is not born as bad as he can be; he is not a beast or demon and therefore his guilt is only more or less intense depending on his own actions, on how he responds to the whisperings of the Holy Spirit (1 Cor. 12.3), to the inner voice of his God-given conscience (Jn. 1.9; Rom. 1.18-20; 2.14-16), and to his understanding of the law of God (Rom. 7.8-13; Jas. 4.17). There exists therefore in and among mankind what may be called "common grace," which enables even sinners to behave rationally and with a certain civility. Men are constantly assisted by grace, even in a sinful state, which enables them to express kindness and do good deeds on a religious or humanitarian level. This is too obvious in history and human experience to require illustration (witness the existence of Roman Catholic hospitals and the charitable works of pagans and sinful men and religious organizations throughout the world); indeed, God's grace cannot be limited in this regard. The Lord has in fact on occasion even helped sinners and idolaters to conform to His will for a temporal purpose (cf. Gen. 20.1-6; 35.5; Ex. 34.24; et al), even Calvin believed this to be so. Yet many Calvinists and other Protestants hold that the image of God in man is so total and intense, that men are altogether without grace to do a good thing, and without a free agency to respond to God to be saved. Both

Luther and Calvin held to the doctrine of the "bondage of the will" and thus denied man's ability to freely accept or reject the offer of salvation---a theology that led to full-blown hyper-Calvinism beginning in the sixteenth century. Yet history, human experience, and the biblical revelation all contradict this doctrine.

The fact that man is free to choose his own way, however, means that he is also free to choose the wrong way. He can spiral downward ever lower in sin, especially through the deceptive powers of Satan. It should be borne in mind, therefore, that, though sin is universal and touches every soul that comes into the world, there are degrees of sin; and this is true regarding both the nature of sin itself and the men who commit sin. Every man therefore is not born necessarily as bad as he can be. Though depravity has the potential to sink men ever deeper in the sewers of filth and degradation (Gen. 6.5; 18.20; 19.24-29; Rom. 1.21-32), and even to make men act like beasts (Dan. 4.31-33; 2 Pet. 2.10-14; Jude 8-13), still some men yield more than others to the propensity to sin. The fact is that some men are more wicked than others. Jesus recognized that Nathaniel was a Jew *"in whom is no guile"* (Jn. 1.47), and Luke mentions the devotion of certain men in the New Testament that, though they were not spiritually regenerated, yet they prayed and gave much alms. Such were the Ethiopian eunuch (Acts 8.26-39) and the Italian band led by Cornelius (10.1-3). They have been labeled as "God-fearers", though it was only after hearing and receiving the Gospel that they were regenerated, sanctified, and Spirit-baptized (10.3-47). Manifestly, some men, even in their fallen state, exemplify a degree of integrity, while others are more wicked and vile. The difference lies in personal choices and the universality and effect of God's grace in response to men of faith on one hand and sinners on the other.

It is argued by Calvinists and others that all imperfections are sin, and anything short of the glory of God in man is sin, even in persons who are saved and live consecrated lives. There may be some element of truth in this in a broad theological sense, and thus, accordingly, all men would do well to pray, *"forgive us of our trespasses."* Nevertheless, "involuntary sin" and "sin in ignorance" (Lev. 4.2; 5.15-19; Num. 15.24; 1 Sam. 14.26-28) are covered in the atonement of Christ, which, according to the passages just cited, is typified in the Old Testament by the atonement of the sacrificial lamb offered up by the priests. Christ, our high priest, has already made atonement for us *"once for all"* in regard to "sins" committed in ignorance or without willful intent (Num. 15.29-31; Heb. 10.10; Is. 53.10; 2 Cor. 5.21; 1 Pet. 2.24). We are therefore sympathetic with Wesley's reasoning on this point, that these are not "sins" in the strict sense of the word. For, though *"[all sin is transgression of the law",* 1 Jn. 3.4] yet not all transgression is sin, at least not in the sense that the person committing the transgression is blameworthy; for he is not doing it willfully and presumptuously or in conscious defiance against God's commandment (Num. 15.27-31).

The Wesleyan view seems supported by Jesus' reasoning in Lu. 12.47-48 in the parable of the servants--- *"And that servant, which knew his lord's will, and prepared not himself, neither did according to his will, shall be beaten with many stripes. But he that knew not, and did commit things worthy of stripes, shall be beaten with few stripes".* Note also Jesus' answer to the Pharisees in Jn. 9.41: *"If ye were blind, ye should have no sin: but now ye say, We see; therefore your sin remaineth".* Add to these words those of James, the Lord's brother: *". . . he that knoweth to do good, and doeth it not, to him it is sin"* (Jas. 4.17). In such cases, we may rest in faith that these "sins" are under the blood of the atoning covenant and will not be laid to our account. Thus David, *"Blessed is the man unto whom the LORD imputes not iniquity."* Only when we become aware of a transgression, do we become personally accountable and blameworthy for it; and thereupon are held accountable to acknowledge and make restitution for that transgression (Lev. 4.1-3; 13-15; 5.1-6, 15-19). We hold therefore that all sin for which a man may be personally guilty and justly blamed and eternally punished is voluntary, that is, sins that are knowingly and deliberately committed, thus disrespecting and defying the will of God (cf. also Rom. 1.20-21, 32; 2.17-27).

Notwithstanding, as shown earlier, the sinner's corrupt nature becomes voluntary at the age of accountability, and it is required of him at that point to respond in faith to God's remedy for it in Christ, who graciously calls men to be reconciled in His love and to freely partake of His holiness (Rom. 3.24; 11.29; 2 Tim. 1.9; 2 Pet. 1.4; Rev. 22.17). We have a moral responsibility at that point to repent and to be wholly sanctified. When the sinner is awakened to his sinfulness and his separation from God, and yet chooses to cling to his depraved nature and to reject the sanctifying power of Christ, he is guilty and blameworthy and must suffer the just punishment for his sinfulness. We see then that a man is not finally condemned and eternally damned for his depravity *per se*, but because he chooses to live in depravity and *"to fulfill the lusts thereof."* So, while the sinner inherits his depravity, he is judged only if he voluntarily keeps it, and thus refuses God's remedy for it in Christ. Thus, *"Likewise reckon ye also yourselves to be dead indeed unto sin, but alive unto God through our Lord Jesus Christ. Let not sin reign in your mortal body"* (Rom. 6.11-12).

Now observe; whether Adam repented of his sin, or not, is of no consequence to anyone else: for *"whosoever shall call on the name of the Lord shall be saved"* (Rom. 10.13; Rev. 22.17). Every man is finally accountable for his own actions (Ezek. 18.4-9, 18-23; Rev. 20.12). It is because we are free to choose Christ and to be transformed by His grace and power that we are also responsible for our state of sinful depravity: for we have free access to God's grace through Christ's atonement and may thus be delivered and made free. To refuse *"so great salvation"* and to willfully and continuously turn away from the Holy Spirit's call to repentance and reconciliation with the Father through His Son is indeed a great scandal and monstrous insult to God.

Observe; Moses "refused" the pleasures of sin and chose rather to suffer affliction with the people of God (Heb. 11.24-25), that is, he "refused" the one and "chose" the other. So, likewise, each one of us is responsible for our actions, whether we choose to remain dead *in Adam* or to be quickened and made alive *in Christ!* (Eph. 2.1-5). Sins spring therefore from a man's depraved lusts and affections acted out of his conscious and personal will (Ezek. 18.19-29; Jas. 4.17; Prov. 9.12). Accordingly, sin is consequentially and finally a deeply personal matter, based upon a conscious act against God and His will, either by commission or omission. This is what makes sin so much more wicked: it is because we know what sin is, by the written Word of God and the illumination of the Holy Spirit, and yet willfully and spitefully indulge in it. Sin is thus *"exceeding sinful"* (Rom. 7.13), which a just and righteous God must necessarily condemn, and finally castaway and punish the sinner who chooses to love and embrace it.

In conclusion, we see that Calvinism is erroneous at its very core, and therefore must be rejected there. It is true that not many today hold to the old five-point Calvinism, yet even "Reformed Calvinism" retains and perpetuates many of the errors of the original system. Our theology begins by articulating the freedom of man to choose, whereas Calvinism begins by articulating the sovereignty of God to determine, which is constructed in a way to allow for sin and to deny the miraculous power of God to instantaneously and entirely sanctify the believer *"in this present world"*, and to perfect him in the image of Christ (Rom. 8.29; 2

Cor. 3.18; Titus 2.12). Indeed, to give an inch to Calvinism in this regard opens the floodgate to other errors; thus, the snake must be severed at the head!

Part 2

Fall of Man, Image of God, and Redemption

We have noticed the revolt and fall of Adam and Eve in Eden against the authority and express commandment of God; and we have argued that the Arminian-Wesleyan interpretation of the fall and its results are truer to Scripture than the Pelagian interpretation on one hand, and the Augustinian-Calvinistic interpretation on the other; for Wesley believed that, though the moral image of God in man was totally lost through Adam, yet at the same time God's eternal decree of atonement in Christ provided the immediate means---the *"free gift"*---to restore that image. Wesley cited many passages to prove his argument, including Gen. 3.15, 20-21; 9.6-17; Rom. 5.12-19; Jn. 1.9; Rom. 8.29-30; 12.3; Eph. 1.4-9; 2 Tim. 1.9-10; Titus 2.11; Rev. 13.8. Contrary to Calvin and his followers, these passages show plainly that man retained a certain likeness to God, even in his fallen state, which enabled him to cooperate with God to be saved; and, as well, it shows that man retained his executive and judicial abilities to establish civil governments and institutions based more or less on God's moral law.

Original Grace Existed Before Original Sin

According to Wesley, God's universal grace in Christ was provided because He anticipated man's fall and graciously foreordained its cure in the Atonement; indeed, He foresaw the fall and thus prescribed man's redemption through the sacrificial *"Lamb slain from the foundation of the world."* The moral benefits and mercies of God were thus co-existent with the fall; in fact, original grace existed before original sin. Accordingly, God prescribed the cure for man's fall before He created Adam; and foresaw all whom down through the ages would accept by faith His gracious pardon and redemption in Christ (Ex. 32.32-34; Dan. 12.1; Eph. 1.4-9, 11-14; 2.5-8; Phil. 4.3; Titus 2.11; Rev. 3.5; 17.8; 19.7-8; 20.12-13, 15).[32]

Many scholars believe that Gen. 3.20-21 is the initial fulfillment of v. 15; namely, that Adam and Eve shortly after their fall were restored to favor with God: for Adam, acting through faith, named his fallen wife, *Eve*, meaning the *"mother of all living"* (v. 20), anticipating apparently her redemption and restoration and thus her status as the "mother" of all who would follow her example in seeking redemption. Further, God made *"coats of skins and clothed them"* (v. 21), an indication that the Lord acknowledged the faith and spiritual restoration of our first parents. The skins that God used presuppose the death of an animal and therefore a blood sacrifice---an atonement that received its authority and power based on the prophetic promise of the spotless *"Lamb slain from the foundation of the world"* (Rev. 13.8).

---

[32] Wesley, *Works*, VI, pp.231-240.

God's Glorious Plan of Redemption and Restoration
Paradise in Christ far Greater than the Paradise of Eden

Some scholars including Wesley assert that God foresaw and thus permitted [not predetermined] the fall and ruin of man so to restore him to a far greater glory and intimacy with God, and to bring about a far greater glory in the world, morally and spiritually.[33] But the greatest witness to this development is the revelation of the apostles and the prophetic Scriptures themselves. John's vision of the *"new heavens and new earth"* far excel anything described in the paradise of Eden. For, among other things that might be noticed, there will be no tempter in the Millennial Reign nor in the new heavens and new earth, and God himself will dwell among the redeemed in a far greater intimacy through the indwelling of the Holy Spirit (Rev. 21.1-27; 22.1-17).

Now read and consider the revelation of the apostle Paul:

> *"According as he hath chosen us in him before the foundation of the world, that we should be holy and without blame before him in love: Having predestined us unto the adoption of children by Jesus Christ to himself, according to the good pleasure of his will, To the praise of the glory of his grace wherein he hath made us accepted in the beloved. In whom we have redemption through his blood, the forgiveness of sins, according to the riches of his grace; Where in he hath abounded toward us in all wisdom and prudence; Having made*

---

[33] Wesley, *Works*, VI, pp. 232-240, 294-296. Calvin believed this also: but his warped view of the sovereignty of God at the expense of man's free agency, and the consequent doctrine of "double predestination" distorted the true Scriptural revelation of the nature of God, including His relationship with man before and after the fall, and His plan of redemption.

known unto us the mystery of his will, according to his good pleasure which he hath purposed in himself . . . In whom also we have obtained an inheritance, being predestinated according to the purpose of him who worketh all things after the counsel of his own will; That we should be to the praise of his glory, who first trusted in Christ. In whom ye also trusted, after that ye heard the word of truth, the gospel of your salvation: in whom also after that ye believed, ye were sealed with that holy Spirit of promise, Which is the earnest of our inheritance until the redemption of the purchased possession, unto the praise of his glory. Wherefore I also, after I heard of your faith in the Lord Jesus, and love unto all the saints" (Eph. 1.4-9, 11-15).

Certainly, the grace of redemption and reconciliation in love with the Father through the Son and in the Holy Spirit could not have been realized without the fall. The glory of Adam's redemption was far greater than his original holiness! And the work of redemption manifested a greater glory and demonstration of God's love and power: for not only did it overturn the rebellion and expectation of Satan to eternally ruin man and mock God, it increased man's blessings and added to God's glory! In this sense, God's infinite wisdom and eternal plan was fulfilled in Christ, and Satan was defeated in his own craftiness.

Wesleyans thus believe not only that all that was lost in Adam may be restored in Christ, but *much more*---namely, deeper intimacy with God and greater appreciation for His grace and mercy, all to the glory of the Father, Son, and Holy Spirit! Orton H. Wiley could not have said it more appropriately nor beautifully in his *Christian Theology*:

"But even the heinousness of his sin and the shame of his fall did not result in his utter destruction . . . The unseen hand of the promised Redeemer prevented it. Thus, the mystery of sin and the mystery of grace met at the gate of Eden".[34]

Genesis 9.7 gives further evidence that God's command to man to *"be fruitful and multiply and replenish the earth"* was not altogether thwarted by the fall; nor that man was so corrupted, as Luther and Calvin purported, that he could not freely respond to the call of God and cooperate with the Lord in His divine plan to save and reconcile men to Himself, and to restore them fully in the image of God. This is shown in vv. 8-17 in his dealings with Noah and his family, and their response to God. Noah's actions plainly were not predetermined by God nor based entirely on a scheme that depended solely on the sovereign grace of God---that is, to the exclusion of man's ability to accept or reject God's gracious offer of redemption. Rather God provided grace for Noah to draw nigh to Him to be saved. Thus Noah *"found grace in the eyes of the Lord"* (6.8). His freedom to choose and ability to reason in faith moved him reverently toward God, and God's grace enabled him to act in obedience to His will: which in turn prompted the favorable response of God (Heb. 11.7; 1 Pet. 3.20; 2 Pet. 2.5). *"Draw nigh to God, and he will draw nigh to you"* (Jas. 4.8). *"Come now, and let us reason together, says the Lord: though your sins be as scarlet, they shall be white as snow"* (Is. 1.18). Indeed, the whole plan of salvation depended on God's grace, but not at the expense of man's integrity and free agency, even in his fallen state; for although man was morally corrupted in the fall, yet he retained his ability to reason and the freedom to choose. For the

---

[34] Orton. H. Wiley, *Christian Theology*, 3 Vols. (Kansas City: Nazarene Publishing house, 1941), II, p. 65.

very idea of commandments and rewards and punishments require a response from creatures endowed with a free moral agency. Else commandments are rendered meaningless, punitive action is unjust, and the concepts of obedience and disobedience make no sense.

It remains here to examine more precisely the results of the fall in view of the "image of God" in human nature. This issue is vigorously debated by theologians and representatives of various religious traditions; and, we admit, there is a degree of mystery that cannot be fully explained. Notwithstanding, the Scriptures are plain enough in revealing that something was not only lost in man in the fall, that is, "original righteousness", but something was added to him, namely, the *"body of sin"* (Rom. 6.6; 7.24; Gal. 5.24; Col. 2.11; 3.5, 9). The intellect, will, and affections of man were marred and impaired, but he now also had a nature inclined toward evil. A sinner repents therefore not only of his actual sins, but of being by nature a sinner, sensing to some degree his deep alienation from God—of being lost and out of fellowship with God: *"Wherefore remember, that ye being in time past Gentiles in the flesh . . . that at that time ye were without Christ, being aliens . . . having no hope, and without God in the world* (Eph. 2.11-12*).* And again, *"Having the understanding darkened, being alienated from the life of God through the ignorance that is in them, because of the blindness of their heart"* (4.18). Sin is therefore both a state and an act. Depravity is a sinful condition of separation and alienation from God and His righteousness, which in turn gives rise to sinful acts.

> *Satan led my soul astray,*
> *From the straight and narrow way.*
> *But to Jesus I did pray,*
> *He heard my prayer,*

Rescued me that very day,
Praise God I'm free,
I've been set free by the grace of God!

Sincere and effectual repentance involves therefore *"godly sorrow"* and the acknowledgment of one's alienation from God. It includes turning away from the evil principle of sin that works toward disobedience. Paul put it like this: *"But I see another law in my members, warring against the law of my mind, and bringing me into captivity to the law of sin which is in my members"* (Rom. 7.23). Observe; this body of sin fosters moral and spiritual corruption. It is the castle and dominion of sin. Paul confesses that this body of corruption had wrought in him covetousness, deceit, and *"all manner of concupiscence [lust]"* (vv.7-11). For this reason, he cried out to be delivered from its power (vv. 24-25).

"Body of Sin"

The body of sin is a cumbersome weight of death and corruption. Fallen man embodies and conceals various kinds of lust---hatred, covetousness, greed, deceit, sensuality. Some see in Paul's image of the body of sin an allusion to an ancient custom in the Greco-Roman world, namely, a sentence of death which certain rulers on occasion would order as fitting punishment for murder. Accordingly, the offender would be bound face to face with the dead body of his victim, and, as such, was forced to carry it about until he fell under the weight and stench of its putrefied mass. Eventually, with his victim starring him in the face, the murderer would die. The account of the Roman poet Virgil (70-19 BC), in his famous work *The Aeneid*, tells of the cursed King Mezentius carrying out the sentence of a convicted murderer.

Till curs'd Mezentius, in a fatal hour,
Assum'd the crown, with arbitrary pow'r.
What words can paint these execrable times,
The subjects' suff'rings, and the tyrant's crimes!
That blood, those murthers, O ye gods, replace,
On his own head, and on his impious race!
The living and the dead at his command
Were coupled, face to face, and hand to hand,
Till, chok'd with stench, in loathed embraces tied,
The ling'ring wretches pin'd away and died.[35]

The Wesleyan commentator, Adam Clark, quotes another translation of Virgil's celebrated poem, which depicts the scene in more colorful language:

What tongue can such barbarities record,
Or count the slaughters of his ruthless sword?
'Twas not enough the good, the guiltless bled,
Still worse, he bound the living to the dead:
These, limb to limb, and face to face, he joined;
O! monstrous crime, of unexplained kind!
Till choked with stench, the lingering wretches lay,
And, in the loathed embraces, died away![36]

Again, we find ourselves in the mainstream of Wesley's thought in this instance, that is, in the view that believers can be delivered completely from depravity and the power of sin, both innate and

---

[35] Publius Virgilius Maro, *The Aeneid*, [John Dryden's Translation]: (Danbury, Conn: Grolier Enterprises Corp., 1909), Book XIII, p. 284: [published as part of The Harvard Classics].

[36] Adam Clark, *Commentary*, 6 Vols. (New York: Abingdon Press, 1832), VI, p. 91.

actual, through God's sanctifying grace and power. We admit, however, that it is difficult to follow and reconcile all of Wesley's views on original sin and its consequences. For he did indeed believe in the universality of racial sin and guilt inherited from Adam, including the consequences of condemnation and eternal punishment.[37] On these points, he admitted that he was only "a hair's breadth from Calvinism." Still, though Wesley believed that men after the fall were born totally depraved with a corruptible *"body of sin"*, and thus deserved eternal retribution, he nevertheless was miles away from Calvin in interpreting how God deals with this "body of sin" in His redemptive plan, and more particularly how men deal with it. For he believed that God had graciously allowed for a "preventing grace" among men based on Christ's ultimate sacrifice on the Cross, which opened to all men, beginning with fallen Adam and Eve, the door to the *"free gift"* of God's universal grace. Further, he did not believe that the fall stripped man completely of the natural image of God, or the "political image" as he called it; by which he meant the ability of men to govern the world and to coexist by God's grace with others in a certain civility and benevolent manner; nor did he believe that fallen man was incapable of doing a good thing.

Like the apostle Paul, Wesley saw God as the *"God of all grace"* triumphing over the Augustinian-Calvinistic concept of God which tended to leave man as the object of His wrath and vengeance. Rather, even under the fall, the Lord *"hath dealt to every man [a] measure of faith"* (Rom. 12.3), and *"the grace of God that bringeth salvation hath appeared to all men, teaching us that, denying ungodliness and worldly lusts, we should live soberly, righteously, and godly in this present world"* (Titus 2.11-

---

[37] Wesley, *Original Sin,* pp. 141-144; *Works*: VI, pp. 215-235.

12). He did indeed see the horribleness of the offence of Adam and its penalty, but he saw *"more much the grace of God, and the gift by grace, which by . . . Jesus Christ hath abounded unto many"* (Rom. 5.15). He saw the power of sin, especially as it abounded under the law, but Wesley was elevated by the Spirit of revelation to see that *"the reign of grace . . . did much more abound"* (v. 20).[38] Again, he acknowledged the justice and righteousness of God and the high standard of holiness to which we are all called: and thus, like James, the Lord's brother, he concluded that for this same reason God *"giveth more grace . . . to the humble"* (Jas. 4.6).

Vision of Christ's Atonement
and Universal Grace

Having therefore the atonement of Christ always in view, the Lord enabled men to form and execute benevolent social agencies and humane institutions, and to establish civil governments in the nations on earth: but all these were always with a view to restore man in the moral image and holiness of God. Consequently, unlike Calvin, Wesley did not see the image of God so intensely mutilated or vitiated that man was no longer human; rather, man retained the ability to reason and the freedom to choose, and thus was made accountable for his actions. He held, moreover, that although the moral image of God in man was destroyed, still, man was not left totally devoid of God's grace. Contrariwise, God remained with man in a certain sense (Jn. 1.9; Rom. 5.15-21), enabling him to respond freely to His merciful plan of salvation in Christ: for Jesus was *"the Lamb slain from the foundation of the world"* (Rev. 13.8); slain for the salvation of every man, with the promise to

---

[38] Wesley, *New Testament*, 2, pp. 338-339. Notes on Rom. 5.12-21.

impart saving grace to everyone who believes and calls upon the name of the Lord (Mk. 16.16; Jn. 3.16; Acts 16.31; Heb. 11.1-40). The atonement of Christ anticipated man's fallen predicament and held back God's fiercest and final wrath: for, though men are born *"the children of wrath"*, yet the Lord is gracious and *"longsuffering toward [men], not willing that any should perish but that all come to repentance"* (2 Pet. 3.9).

> *Sweet is the song I am singing today;*
> *I'm redeemed! I'm redeemed!*
> *Trouble and sorrow have vanished away*
> *I have been redeemed!*
> *Great is my joy now as onward I go;*
> *I'm redeemed! I'm redeemed!*

Wesley based his thinking along these lines on many Scriptural passages, for example, *"That [Christ] was the true Light, which lights every man that comes into the world"* (Jn. 1.9). Accordingly, even sinners have within and/or about them a certain grace that enables them to be enlightened to the righteousness and goodness of God, with the ability to respond freely in faith to His righteousness and goodness (Lu. 3.6; Jn. 3.16-17; Rom. 5.18; 1 Tim. 2.4; 2 Tim. 2.1-5; Titus 2.11-12; 2 Pet. 3.9). For this same reason, however, he believed that since each man is born free to accept or reject God's gracious redemption, he must also bear the burden for his decisions and actions, and therefore must finally be judged on his own record. A man therefore ultimately chooses eternal life and/or everlasting death (Deut. 30.19; Josh. 24.15; Prov. 1.23-30). In the final analysis, therefore, sin and eternal judgment are deeply personal matters.

On this point, Wesley stood in stark contradiction to Calvin: for "preventing grace," as Wesley called it, not only enabled sinners to respond in faith to God's redemptive plan, but kept them, or prevented them, if they were willing, from being as bad as they could be. More importantly, it put no limits on God's grace to save and restore all men perfectly in the moral image of God, if they were willing. This became the distinctive mark in the Wesleyan proclamation of the Gospel. Whoever was willing could be sanctified and perfectly restored, morally and spiritually, in the divine image. Thus, like Paul, it was far removed from Wesley to *"frustrate the grace of God"* (Gal. 2.21).

Sin in the light of the law,
and in the light of Christ

Sin was exposed for what it is by the law of God (Rom. 4.15; 5.20; 7.8-13); brought to light more fully through the preaching of the prophets (Jer. 3.1, 14; Ezek. 43.5-12; Mal. 3.1-5, 7-18), and still more fully through the life and teachings of Jesus and the apostles (Mt. 5.17-48; 6.1-24; 7.1-14, 21-24, 28-29; Jn. 1.1-17; Acts 2.42; 18.24-28; 2 Cor. 3.6-18; 2 Pet. 3.2; Jude 17). We see especially through Christ and His teachings the very core of sin, as well as the very essence of grace; and, consequently, we see more clearly the judgment of sin. For judgment and wrath were brought to light especially in Jesus' preaching and teaching (Mt. 3.10-12; 8.12; 11.12-13; 21.42-44; 1 Pet. 2.2-8; Rom. 10.6-13, 16-21), that is, sin was completely unmasked and seen for what it is in the revelation of Christ. Again, if sin is the offense and barrier between eternal life and eternal damnation, and if it is to be finally judged we should be diligent to learn what it is (2 Chron. 7.13-22; Ezra 10.11; Is. 56.1; 59.1-15; Dan. 12.2; Mt. 25.31-46; Rom. 2.1-11; 1 Cor. 5.9-10; 6.17; 15.50; Gal. 5.19-21; 2 Thess. 1.7-9; Heb. 7.26; Rev. 20.14; 21.7-8, 27).

Now observe; the law under Moses was *"just, and holy, and good"* (Rom. 7:12), but it was powerless *per se* to deliver men from sin. The law, like a mirror, enables a man to see himself as he really is, that is, it reveals his spots and blemishes and corruptions; yet the mirror is powerless to change him (Jas. 1.23-24). Thus, Paul says, *"where no law is, there is no transgression"* (Rom. 4.15), that is, there is no awareness of transgression. Again, when he says, *"for by the law is the knowledge of sin"* (3.20) and *"the law entered, that the offence might abound"* (5.20), he means the law exposes sin for what it is and manifests the judgment of God against it. Thus, he says, *"But sin, taking occasion by the commandment, wrought in me all manner of concupiscence. For without the law sin was dead. For I was alive without the law once: but when the commandment came, sin revived, and I died"* (7.8-9). He does not mean of course that the law literally wrought sin in him, for *"the law is just and holy,"* rather he means the law exposed his sin---the *"all manner of concupiscence"* seated in his fallen nature. The purpose of the law then is to bring the knowledge of sin, and conviction through that knowledge by the grace and power of the Holy Spirit. Pardon and sanctification come only by grace through faith (Rom. 3.24; Eph. 2.8; 2 Thess. 2.13); therefore, when sin is unmasked by the law, and the sinner does not deal with it in sincere repentance through grace and faith, it causes a deepening of sin in him, with various proliferating manifestations (Gal. 5.19-21; 1 Cor. 6.9; Eph. 5.5; Col. 3.5; Rev. 21.8).

We have seen that the law is powerless to do anything but to manifest sin and God's judgment against it. In fact, to endeavor to live by the law of Moses, without being in Christ, can only produce legalism, hypocrisy, and a curse (Mt. 5.20-48; 6.1-18; Gal. 3.10-12): for it is impossible to keep the letter of that law, for the same reason that it is impossible to go through life without breaking some trivial law contrived by men: for the law of Moses was *"contrary to us"* (Col. 2.14), and its ceremonial ordinances were to *"perish with the using"* (3.22). Moreover, if we break the law at any point, we to break it at every point (Jas. 2.10); and thus, if a new and better covenant had not been made in Christ (Heb. 8.7-13; 9.11-12), everyone would have necessarily perished: for it is impossible to keep all the law under the terms of the Old Testament. Therefore, the beloved apostle says, *"For the law was **given by** Moses, but grace and truth **came by** Jesus Christ"* (Jn. 1.17).

Leaven of Hypocrisy

The predicament of the Pharisees and their *"leaven of . . . hypocrisy"* (Lu. 12.1) was that they endeavored to keep every precept of the ceremonial law, an effort impossible of itself, and, more importantly, an effort that prevented them from receiving Christ by faith and being recreated in the image of God. Their effort produced in them the only thing that it could: an obnoxious boasting in self-righteousness and hypocrisy (Mt. 5.20; 6.1-5, 16-18; 7.3-5; 23.13, 28; Rev. 3.16; see also Amos 5.21-24). But this is the result always when one attempts to keep religious laws and ceremonies contrived by men: for they inevitably supplant the grace of Christ and God's perfect law. It produces always merely a cover for legalism and self-righteousness and generates artificial standards of righteousness. In fact, grace both empowers the believer for righteousness and enables him to discern through the Spirit the will of God.

The cry of the Spirit in both Old and New Testaments is thus: *"Circumcise yourselves to the Lord, take away the foreskin of your hearts"* (Jer. 4.4; 9.26; Rom. 2.29; Col. 2.11; Phil. 3.3): for when the heart is cleansed, and true fellowship is restored with God, the saint desires only to please the Lord in all things and to keep His commandments. Thus, Paul says, *"the law is not made for a righteous man"* (1 Tim. 1.9): for a righteous man is governed by the indwelling of the Spirit of God, who conditions and modifies the heart to delight in pleasing the Lord in all things. Only *faith that works by love* can produce a submissive spirit and heartfelt obedience to Christ, and thus keep the believer blameless before the Lord (Rom. 1.17; 3.22-28; 5.1-2; 16.26; 1 Cor. 2.5; Gal. 3.12-26; Col. 1.23; Heb. 3.6, 14).

Christ, our Schoolmaster

The law fulfilled itself as a *paidagogos*, which in biblical times was a "tutor" or "guide" who took the child to school, and thus, accordingly, not the teacher *per se*. The law was thus *paidagogos humon eis Christon, "our tutor to bring us to Christ"* (Gal. 3.24-25; cp. 1 Cor. 4.15); which our KJV unfortunately translates as "schoolmaster" in Gal. 3.24. In any case, upon arriving at Christ, men have in Him all they need for salvation and righteousness: for He is *"made unto us wisdom, and righteousness, and sanctification, and redemption"* (1 Cor. 1.30; see also Is. 2.3; 9.6-7; Jer. 23.5). Christ's life and actions on earth were the personification and demonstration of God's law. He himself was God and the truth! Moses' legislation was thus *"nailed to the cross"* with Christ; God thus *"took it out of the way"* (Col. 2:14): for it had merely a temporal purpose. Jesus was *"made a curse for us"* (Gal. 3.13), effectively removing through His atoning sacrifice the *"curse of the law,"* and giving us new life in Him! Indeed, *"[He] is our life"* (Col. 3.4). Even the pagan poet somehow discerned that *"in him we live, and move, and have our being"* (Acts 17.28).

"Royal Law" versus
"Carnal Commandments"

Now observe; the eternal law of God, the *"perfect law of liberty"* (Jas. 1.25; 2.12), the *"royal law"* (2.8), the *"law of faith"* (Rom. 3.27), *the law of love* (Gal. 5.14), *"the law of Christ"* (6.2), in contrast with the law of Moses, corresponds perfectly to the true nature and will of God. This is the law that Paul says is *"spiritual"* (Rom. 7.14); whereas Moses' law was composed of many *"carnal commandments"* and *"carnal ordinances"* (Heb. 7.16; 9.10) that were contrary to the *"new man"* born of grace and the Spirit of God. The law of liberty, the Gospel, is the perfect law that *"converts the soul"* (Ps. 19.7); it is the law in which the new creature in Christ delights and rejoices! It is the *"law of the Spirit of life in Christ"* (Rom. 8.2). Paul's aim was thus to teach and train ministers to be *"able ministers of the new covenant"* (2 Cor. 3.6; Col. 1.25-29).

The Gospel contains therefore a system of laws and commandments conditioned by grace and ordained from the foundation of the world (1 Cor. 15.10; 2 Cor. 3.6; Eph. 1.18-19; 2.5-7, 13; 3.2-5; Heb. 8.6-13; 12.24); a system that corresponds perfectly with the new heart we receive in Christ (Ps. 40.8; Jer. 31.31-34; 32.38-40; Ezek. 11.19-20; 2 Cor. 3.2-3), which enables us to delight in Christ and His will. In fact, the law of God under grace is a higher and stricter standard of righteousness in that it requires our very thoughts to be in harmony with the holiness of God (Mt. 5.20-48). Paul thus says that, though he was without the law of Moses, yet he was not without law to God, *"but under the law of Christ"* (1 Cor. 9.20-21). God's law under grace flows like a river out of the heart of sanctified men---men transformed and empowered by the indwelling of the Spirit of God. It is only on this basis that John could say, *"For this is the love of God, that we keep his commandments: and his commandments are not grievous"* (1 Jn. 5.3). In fact, the *faith that works by love* discerns what is true, knows the difference between God's law and the doctrines of men, judges all in the light of the Gospel and the indwelling Spirit of God, and gives believers a new heart to delight in the commandments of God. Consecrated saints *"delight in the law of God after the inward man"* (Rom. 7.22). Like David they exclaim, *"O how I love thy law!"* (Ps. 119.97), and they rejoice to do His will and to keep His commandments (vv. 16, 24, 43-50, 92).

Jesus' Teaching on Sin

Jesus, our Savior and Lord is also our primary Teacher (Mt.7.28-29; Jn. 16.13-14). All the law and prophets are to be understood from the standpoint of His interpretations and teachings. Therefore, the final rule of faith and practice for the church is, *"But I [Christ] say unto you . . ."* (Mt. 5.17-48). This is in part what Jesus meant in saying, *"I am Alpha and Omega, the beginning and the ending"* (Rev. 1.8), and what Paul means by *"Christ is the end of the law for righteousness"* (Rom. 10.4), and what the writer of Hebrews signifies by calling Jesus the *"author and finisher of our faith"* (Heb. 12.2), namely, that the true *"church of the living God"* is built up from the standpoint of the Chief Cornerstone, both in our Lord's personal example of righteousness and in His teachings. Even when the eternal law of God (in contrast with the temporal aspects of Moses' law) was seen for what it was by inspired prophets under the Old Covenant, still it was grasped in the main only with a surface knowledge. It remained for the deeper significance of God's eternal law to be brought to light by Christ and the apostles (Lu. 10.24; Eph. 3.2-5; 1 Pet. 1.10-12; Heb. 10.1-16).

Now, observe; Jesus and the apostles separated the ceremonial aspects of the law from the *"royal law"* of the Gospel; and established the church upon the eternal and spiritual principles of that law. The former laws--- *"touch not; taste not; handle not"* (Col. 2.21) were *"nailed to the cross"* with Christ; and, significantly, remained buried with Him though He himself was resurrected (vv. 14-15). The ceremonial laws were done away with in Christ: for they had no true moral value. In fact, they were *"carnal"* (Heb. 7.16), the *"commandments and doctrines of men"* (Col. 2.22), having been instituted because the people's hearts had become hardened by sin (Mt. 19.3-8). In other words, Moses' law was instituted to deal with the people as sinners, not as saints (1Tim. 1.9). But once Christ came on the scene in God's plan, the *"rudiments"* and *"weak and beggarly elements"* of the Mosaic system came to an end, having served their purpose (Gal. 4.9-10; Col. 2.8, 20; Heb. 7.11-28; 8.1-13).

We see then that Christ fully illuminated what sin is and laid out for us how to deal with it. The apostles fleshed out Jesus' teachings through the inspiration of the Holy Ghost. In their words and teachings, we have the full and complete revelation of the will of God (Mt. 5.17-19; Jn. 5.39; 16.13-14; Acts 2.42; Rom. 3.31; Eph. 1.9-13; 2.20; 3.1-5; 2 Tim. 3.15-17; 1 Pet. 1.10-12; 2 Pet. 1.3, 20; 3.2). Through Christ and the apostles, the true meaning of the law was brought forth and established (Mt. 5.17; Rom. 3.31).

Accordingly, our covenant pledge in Zion Assembly states that we take the whole Bible rightly divided: but we emphasize that the New Testament is *our rule of faith, practice, government, and discipline.* By this we mean simply that we interpret the whole Bible in the light of Christ and the New Covenant. We see sin therefore, like Christ and the apostles did: not against the ceremonial aspects of the law, but in the light of the moral power of God's eternal law to convert and transform sinners into the image of Christ, in *"true grace"* and *"true holiness"* (Eph. 4.24; 1 Pet. 5.12). This is what James, the Lord's brother, calls the *"royal law"* (Jas. 2.8). It is the *law of Christ,* the law of King Jesus! It is the revelation of the perfect will of God; the eternal Word of God written in our hearts and planted deeply into our consciences by the Holy Spirit (Jer. 31.31-33; 32.40; Ezek. 11.19-20; 36.26-27; 2 Cor. 3.2-3; Heb. 8.8-10; 10.16; Rev. 21.3).

Darkness of Sin Exposed
Against the Light of Divine Love

Jesus' teachings showed up the darkness of sin like a silhouette against the light of divine love---love that is gracious, kind, true, and charitable (Mt. 22.40; Lu. 10.25-37; Jn. 3.16-18; 15.9-10; 17.26). The apostles' teachings likewise see sin against the glistening light of divine love, which God graciously imparted to men in the Holy Spirit, enabling them to fellowship together in His love and truth (Rom. 13.8, 10; 1 Cor. 13; Gal. 5.14; 1 Jn. 3.11; 4.7-12). The *law of Christ* is thus always ethical and moral, corresponding to the heart and holy character of God. It empowers the believer to act and react in love, and thus to always please the Lord: for love *"never fails."* Pharisees, legalists, and religionists, on the other hand, see sin more as the breaking of certain rules and regulations invented by the traditions of men (Mt. 5.16-48; 6.1-34; 7.1-12). Jesus despised this kind of religiosity, particularly because it inevitably negates or diminishes the true commandments of God and His infinite wisdom (Mt. 15.1-9; 16.6-12; Mk. 12.28-34; cp. with 1 Sam. 15.22; Hos. 6.6; Amos 5.21; Mic. 6.6-8). He reprimanded carnal religiosity as hypocrisy, knowing that it is nothing more than a spiritually empty *"form of godliness,"* a pretense of righteousness without true moral power.

Our Lord therefore established the church upon a law and conduct inspired by the love of God, which is *"shed abroad in our hearts by the Holy Ghost"* (Mt. 5.46; Jn. 13.35; 15.12, 13, 17; 17.26; see also Rom. 12.9; 13.10; 1 Cor. 13; Heb. 13.1; 1 Pet.1.22; 1 Jn. 4.7-10, 21); that is, He desired the church's behavior to be motivated by and grounded in divine love, which corresponds always to God's holiness and truth. Thus, the kind of conduct of which the Lord approves grows out of divine love that ends in holiness. It may be seen that there is therefore no tension between God's true law and pure love (Mt. 5.17-20; Jn. 14.15, 21-23; 15.10, 14; 1 John 5.3). His love in fact inspires a conformity to His righteousness, and *"rejoices in the truth"* (1 Cor. 13.6). True righteousness is therefore understood only from the perspective of loving God with all of one's heart, mind, soul, and strength, and loving our neighbors as ourselves (Mt. 7.12, 22, 37-39).

The Unforgivable Sin
"Blasphemy against the Holy Ghost"

The phrase, *"blasphemy against the Holy Ghost,"* which Jesus used in His teaching about the kingdom of God (Mt. 12.24-32), has generated varied opinions and much controversy. Our view is based on the following observations: *First*, the description can hardly signify some particularly wicked sin, as a thing in and of itself; and, thus, that it denotes a sin more wicked than all others, and is therefore unforgivable. For this would be contradictory to several biblical teachings that magnify God's grace and His infinite mercy, and His readiness to forgive anyone who repents; including forgiveness of the most vile and heinous of sins, even sins against God's name and honor (Ps. 74.10-12; Is. 52.5; Ezek. 36.20-33; Jas. 2.7-13; and compare with Is. 1.18; Mic. 7.18-19; Mt. 11.19; 12.31, 32; 1 Tim. 1.13). *Second,* since the glory and power of the kingdom belong to God and Christ (Mt. 6.10, 13; Col. 1.13; 1 Cor. 15.24; Rev. 12.10), blasphemy against the Holy Ghost can hardly mean some peculiar blasphemy against the Holy Ghost in contradistinction to blasphemies uttered against the Father and the Son. For if God is willing to forgive blasphemies against Christ and against His own majestic name and honor, He is willing also to forgive blasphemies against the name and honor of the Holy Spirit. In fact, He says in this same place, *"All manner of sin and blasphemy shall be forgiven men"* (v. 31). *Third,* we have evidence that some of the very Pharisees whom Jesus was addressing in this passage and elsewhere, later repented of their blasphemy and were forgiven. One of them particularly seems enough to satisfy our point here. This fierce and zealous Pharisee was named, Saul. He was a leader and representative of the teaching and spirit of this sect of Judaism, and a typical blasphemer who denied the basic truths of the Gospel, including the fact that God has a Son. And he also attributed the work of the Spirit to demons. This blasphemer was wonderfully saved by the same power that he had before so vehemently denied (Acts 7.51-8.1; 9.1-18; Gal. 1.13).

This violent zealot and terrorist named Saul became none other than our apostle Paul. He, as much as anyone who ever lived, proves the immensity of God's grace and His patience and infinite mercy. In his own testimony, he says, *"And I thank God through Jesus Christ our Lord, who has enabled me, for that he counted me faithful, putting me in the ministry. Who was before a blasphemer, and a persecutor, and injurious: but I obtained mercy, because I did it ignorantly in unbelief"* (1 Tim. 1.12-13). And he continues in vv. 14-17 to magnify the *"exceeding abundance"* of God's grace *"with faith and love,"* endeavoring to assure all that *"Christ*

Jesus came into the world to save sinners. " Further, we have heard in our ministry men and women speak vile things against the work of the Holy Ghost who later repented and were saved.

A celebrated minister in the early part of the last century is reported to have uttered one of the most insidious blasphemies against the Holy Spirit, calling the Pentecostal movement "the last vomit of Satan." Another said, "I would rather see a poisonous viper come in among my sheep than a tongues-talking Pentecostal." Many have made similarly foolish and blasphemous statements such as these; yet later repented and were Spirit-baptized themselves and became useful in the work of the Lord.

Understanding Jesus' meaning in Mt. 12.24-32, Mk. 3.28-30, Lu. 12.10 is plainly connected with His teaching regarding the immediate ushering in of the kingdom of God, which He demonstrated by His power to cast out demons. Now observe: Jesus attributed both the truth of His teaching and His ability to cast out devils to the dynamic work of the Holy Ghost (Lu. 4.18; Jn. 1.32; 3.34-36; 5.19, 30; 6:36-39; 7.16-18; 8.29). His meaning of the phrase *"blasphemy against the Holy Ghost"* thus seems to be this: he who speaks against and harbors in his heart unbelief and defiance against the work of the Spirit in revealing God, either outwardly or inwardly, without repentance, will be eternally damned and tormented in hell. The same idea is conveyed in Proverbs. *"He, that being often reproved hardens his neck, shall be destroyed, and that without remedy"* (Prov. 29.1). And this is true of anyone who may otherwise seem morally good, religious, and does charitable deeds. In other words, one may conform his life to a certain religious creed, like the Pharisees did, or live by the social norms adopted by the world, and thus stand justified before men; but if he persists to ignore and reject the pleadings of Holy Spirit, refuses the gracious offer of the Lord to become a new creature in Christ (Jn. 3.3-8, 36), and thereby defiles his own conscience which bears witness in the Holy Spirit, his inner self will continuously degenerate into ungodliness and further alienation from God. *"Ye stiffnecked and uncircumcised in heart and ears, ye do always resist the Holy Ghost: as your fathers did, so do ye . . . and they have slain them which [showed] before of the coming of the Just One; of whom ye have been now the betrayers and murderers: Who have received the law by the disposition angels and have not kept it"* (Acts 7.51). This is what we see in Israel's resistance to God, which provoked His wrath and finally caused Him *to "cut them off"* and destroy them (Ex. 32.9; 33.3; Is. 48.4; Jer. 4.4; 6.10-11; Heb. 3.7-12, 15-19).

We can see then that it is very dangerous to trifle with God! The least bit of resistance to Him can harden one's heart and make one even more resistant to God. Many have been turned into counterfeits and reprobates by *"always resisting the Holy Ghost"* (Acts 7.51-58). Behold, it is a *"fearful thing to fall into the hands of the living God"* (Heb. 10.31): for *Jehovah*, not man, is ultimately the one *"with whom we have to do"* (4.13). Thus, Jesus said, *"Be not afraid of them that kill the body, and after they have no more that they can do. But I forewarn you whom you shall fear: Fear him, which after he has killed has power to cast into hell"* (Lu. 12.4-5).

Now, observe; blaspheming against the Holy Ghost is set over against blaspheming and speaking evil against Christ and God because it is the office work of the Holy Ghost to reveal God and His Son: and the Spirit does this in a more effective way than the Son while the latter was in the world (Jn. 16.7-15). For, unlike Christ in the flesh, the Holy Ghost speaks and reveals God and His truth to a man's conscience and inner spirit in a more dynamic way than either the Father or the Son. To put it another way, it is the office and agency of the Holy Spirit to reveal and perform the will of the whole Godhead. Moreover, the Spirit draws men to Christ and God, and thus men more particularly and intimately resist Him. See here; Jesus during His earthly ministry spoke to the outward ear of men, whereas the Spirit speaks more intimately to the inner ear. Accordingly, the Holy Ghost is called the *Spirit of truth.* Thus, Jesus said, *"It is expedient that I go away: for if I go not away, the Comforter will not come unto you . . . And when he is come, he will reprove the world of sin"* (Jn. 16.7-8); and again, *"Howbeit when he, the Spirit of truth, is come . . . he shall not speak of himself; but whatsoever he shall hear that shall he speak: and he will show you things to come. He shall glorify me: for he shall receive of mine, and shall show it unto you. All things that the Father has are mine: therefore, I said, that he shall take of mine, and shall show it unto you"* (vv. 13-15). We see, then, the distinctive work of the Holy Spirit in the Godhead: for *"no man can say that Jesus is Lord, but by the Holy Ghost"* (1 Cor. 12.3).[39]

We conclude, therefore, that for one to continuously reject and defy the Spirit's revelation of God in Christ, and to continuously resist His convicting power, will in the end incur the wrath of God. This seems to be the meaning of Jesus' words in Mt. 12.31-32; namely, that such a hateful and rebellious disposition against a pleading God is nothing less than *"blasphemy against the Holy Ghost,"* a state of being that *"shall not be forgiven . . . in this world, [nor] in the world to come."*

---

[39] An article by Patrick H. Alexander, "Blasphemy Against the Holy Spirit", in Stanley M. Burgess and Gary B. McGee, editors, *Dictionary of Pentecostal and Charismatic Movements* (Grand Rapids: Zondervan Publishing House, 1988), pp. 87-89 offers an insightful treatment of this subject. His conclusion based on a work by J. Jeremias, *New Testament Theology: The Proclamation of Jesus*, captures in a kernel the essential meaning of Jesus words in Mt. 12.32, to wit, that the "the unforgiveable sin is not a particular moral transgression . . . rather it is the sin that arises in connection with revelation", which is to say, the continual resistance and rejection of the Holy Spirit revealing the goodness and saving grace of Christ and the sinner's need of reconciliation and cleansing.

See here: if the greatest commandment is to *love God with all of one's heart, mind, soul, and strength*, then the greatest sin must be to refuse to love God with all of one's heart: for God has poured Himself out to men in unspeakable grace and self-humiliation in Christ, to save and reconcile man. It is therefore an unspeakable and unforgiveable evil to constantly ignore and reject His gracious offer in Christ. Think of it! *"Behold, what manner of love the Father has bestowed upon us"* (1 Jn. 3.1); *"For God so loved the world that he gave his only begotten"* (v. 16); *"God was in Christ, reconciling the world unto himself"* (2 Cor. 5.19). Rejection and/or denial of such a gracious and explicit revelation of God can only meet finally with His rejection and just punishment---the "second death", eternal separation from God and everlasting damnation.

Think of what an impact it has upon the Creator and Master of the universe when men stubbornly and persistently refuse His gracious offer to pardon, reconcile, and cleanse men through the sacrifice of His only begotten Son. *"He that . . . believeth not the Son shall not see life; but the wrath of God abides on him"* (Jn. 3.36). But observe; the extreme wickedness of unbelief is seen more particularly in the light of the ministry of the Holy Spirit: for it is through His special agency that the love of God is manifested and shed abroad in men's hearts; indeed, He is the revealing and reconciling agent of the Godhead (Jn. 16.7, 12-15; Rom. 5.5, 8; 1 Cor. 2.1-16; 12.3; 1 Jn. 3.24; 4.9, 10, 13).

Now the Pharisees to whom Jesus was ministering were in jeopardy of doing this very thing, that is, of rejecting the outpouring of God's love in Christ, especially as His love was being revealed by the demonstrative power of the Holy Spirit. Further, they attributed Jesus' anointed teaching and power to an *"unclean spirit"* (Mk. 3.30). But, again, are we to believe that the Pharisees were condemned for all eternity for their denial of Christ on this occasion? Obviously not, for we have already noticed that some were later forgiven and became outstanding witnesses and ministers for the Lord. In fact, Jesus speaks in this very place not in a way to finally judge the Pharisees, but to warn them, as if to say, "If you continue in your stubborn and obstinate refusal to believe in me, especially now that the Father himself has manifested His approval of me through the Holy Spirit (Jn. 8.23-55), you will be eternally damned (5.17, 19-24; 10.36-38; 14.10-13). Jesus was reasoning and pleading with them to repent and believe the Gospel, and at the same time warning them of the tragic consequences of persistent unbelief (Mt 12.33-37). Mark adds in his account of Jesus' warning against this blasphemy, that the unbelievers are *"in danger of eternal damnation"* (Mk. 3.28). Obstinate unbelief is therefore the *"unforgivable sin"* (Acts 4.7-12, 15-19; 5.3-5; 7.51-53; Heb. 3.12, 19; 4.6, 11; Rev. 21.8).

We see then that blasphemy against the Holy Ghost is set over against repentance and is equated with obstinate unbelief. This is the essence of Jesus' parables in Mt. 21.28-40. Many publicans and harlots blasphemed the Spirit, but later repented and were accepted by the Lord (v. 29). But the scribes and Pharisees in general refused to believe in Christ and repent (vv. 31-32). The end of their blasphemy was this: the kingdom of God was taken from them (v. 43); and thus the Son of God, the *"the stone which the builders rejected,"* must in the end *"grind [them] to powder"* (v. 44). Observe, when sinners refuse to repent, they are refusing to acknowledge and yield to the grace and goodness of God, which is revealed in Christ in a special way through the Holy Spirit (Gen. 6.3; Acts 7.51; Heb. 3.7; Rom. 2.4; 2 Cor. 7.10). They resist with stubborn defiance the pleadings of the sweet Heavenly Dove, who is sent to *"reprove the world of sin"* and to reveal the grace and glory of the Father in Christ (Jn. 16.7-15). Men are drawn to God through the peculiar work of the Holy Spirit (Rom. 8.8-9, 14-16); they are justified and sanctified through Him (Jn. 3.5-8; 2 Thess.

2.13; 1 Pet. 1.2) and are sealed by His authority and power (2 Cor. 1.22; Eph. 1.13-14; 1 Pet. 1.5). To receive Him is to receive the Father and the Son, and to reject Him is to reject the Father and the Son; for God is a trinity (Jn. 1.1, 14, 18; Rom. 8.9-11, 26-28; Eph. 4.4-6; Col. 2.9; 1 Jn. 5.7).

The "Purgatory" Fiction

We see then that for men to continually resist the special work of the Spirit of God in calling them to repentance and reconciliation with God is blasphemy against Him---a condition and state of being that, if maintained, negates the possibility of forgiveness *"in this world, [and] in the world to come"* (Mt. 12.31-32): for if sin is not forgiven in this world, it will not be forgiven in the next: indeed, contrary to the Roman Catholic fiction of "purgatory," there is no second chance after this life, and no purging after death. The repentant thief on the cross went immediately to Paradise after he died; he did not go through "purgatory" (Lu. 23.43; see also 16.22-31; Heb. 9.27; see also Is. 66.24; Mk. 9.43-47; 2 Cor. 6.2; Rev. 20.12-15). The only "purgatory" is in this present life; and the purging agent is the Holy Spirit (2 Thess. 2.13; 1 Pet. 1.2), and the purging element is the blood of Christ (Heb. 9.22; 12.24; 1 Pet. 1.2, 19; 1 Jn. 1.7; Rev. 1.5; 5.9). *"For he says . . . behold, now is the accepted time; behold, now is the day of salvation"* (2 Cor. 6.2). *"And as it is appointed unto men once to die, but after this the judgment"* (Heb. 9.27; see also 2 Cor. 5.10; Rev. 20.12-13). After death, the sinner and ungodly indeed will burn, but they will not be purged! The lake of fire is not for purification but for vindication of divine wrath and eternal punishment.

A Right View of Imputation

We have noticed some of the more serious errors of Calvinism. The interpretation of *imputation* in by Calvinists is another one of them (cf. Rom. 4.6, 11, 22-24; 5.13; Jas. 2.23; 2 Cor. 5.19). Contrary to Calvin and those under the influence of his teachings, Christ's personal righteousness is not imputed to believers any more than Adam's personal sin in Eden was imputed to his descendants, at least not in the sense of Adam's personal guilt with its eternal consequences and punishment. True, it is said that our Lord bore our sins and iniquities, and in fact that God *"made Him to be sin for us"* (Is. 53.4-6, 10-12; 2 Cor. 5.21): but this does not equate with the idea that Christ committed our sins or that He was guilty of doing so; nor that He was eternally punished for doing so. Jesus was simply *"our scapegoat"* (Lev. 16.10, 21-22; Heb. 9.28). True, He suffered for us, and God *"laid upon Him the iniquities of us all"* (Is. 53.3-6): and in this sense, it may be said that our sins were imputed to Him; but it is always that a man is either eternally rewarded or eternally condemned for his own moral conduct, not for another's. No one's sinfulness can be charged up against or credited to another with blame and just punishment, particularly not eternal punishment. But again, as we have noticed elsewhere, one may indeed endure temporal sufferings in association with what another has done. Our inherited depravity because of Adam's transgression in Eden, with its spiritual and temporal death and deranged conditions on earth, including in the hearts of men, is sufficient proof of this fact.

But to claim that all men since Adam have somehow committed Adam's sin and therefore Adam's personal sin is also the personal sin of all men is an absurd fiction. It is a doctrine more akin to some Eastern cults and religious traditions than to the teachings of Christ and the apostles. It is the nonsense that Augustine conjured up and spread in the fifth century, the same which Calvin revived and perpetuated in the sixteenth, namely, that we all sinned in Adam and therefore incur the guilt for it along with the penalty of eternal death and damnation. We have seen also that some Calvinists teach that all men sinned in Adam before they were even born. This idea is more akin to Plato, Origen, and Manichaeism than to the teachings of Christ and the apostles!

According to this same faulty interpretation of imputation, it is asserted that Christ's personal righteousness is imputed to believers (thus the erroneous and misleading term *imputed righteousness*), rather than the spirit and principle of God's righteousness being *imparted* to us through faith. The mistaken idea of "imputed righteousness" occasions spurious conversions and regeneration [see below]. It has given rise to the sayings, "I am a sinner saved by grace" and "saved sinners." For it assumes that sinners are justified on the merits of Christ's righteous life, that is, that Christ's righteousness is ascribed to unregenerate men; thus, the sinner is "as if" he is living righteous though he is really living in sin. This is nothing more than nonsense and *"another Gospel!"*

> *Search me O God, and know my heart today;*
> *Try me, O Savior, know my thoughts I pray;*
> *See if there be some wicked way in me;*
> *Cleanse me from every sin and set me free.*

The Calvinistic view of imputation contradicts and negates the plain teaching of Scripture, particularly because to be justified we *must* be "born again" and become a new creature in Christ through the transforming power of the Holy Spirit (Jn. 3.3-8; Rom. 12.2; Col. 1.13). Justification is therefore not merely forensic (as Luther and Calvin taught), it is actual! *"Therefore, if any man be in Christ, he is a new creature: old things are passed away and, behold, all things are become new"* (2 Cor. 5.17); and *"if any man have not the Spirit of Christ, he is none of his"* (Rom. 8.9); and again, *"The Spirit itself beareth witness with our spirit, that we are the children of God"* (v. 16).

The teachings of the Scriptures on this subject, seen together as a whole and rightly divided show plainly that God does not justify sinners based on the imputation of Christ's personal righteousness; for, according to this heresy, God overlooks the sins of sinners who believe, seeing in them the righteousness of Christ: and He justifies them on this basis, overlooking their transgressions. As such, it is asserted that believers stand positionally righteous before God, rather than being spiritually transformed by His grace and thus enabled to live a truly righteous life. The idea of a positional righteousness in Christ without becoming really a new creature is a "damnable heresy." For, if men are saved by Christ's righteousness, there would have been no need for Him to have died: for Jesus was righteous before He died. Rather, it is made plain that we are justified by His death through grace and faith (Rom. 5.1-8; Eph. 2.8). *"Jesus died for our sins"* (1 Cor. 15.3; see also Is. 53.5-6, 10), that is, He died to effectively remove our sins, not to overlook them! (Jn. 1.29; Rom. 6.1-7; 7.23-24; 8.1-11).

The truth is that men are saved by being spiritually transformed by faith into Christ's likeness through His death (Heb. 9.22; 10.19; 12.24; 1 Pet. 1.19; 1 Jn. 1.7; Rev. 1.5; 5.9); not by Christ's righteousness *per se,* but by His power to create us anew in His holiness. Thus, by grace through faith we become righteous. Jesus does not obey God for us; we must of our own free will obey Him. This proves our love for Him (Jn. 14.21, 23-24; 15.9-11; 1 Cor. 7.19; 1 Jn. 2.4; 3.24). Jesus does not live holy for us, He empowers us to live holy. He is not vicariously our righteousness; rather He transforms us by faith into His righteousness.

It is true that Jesus' willingness to die in our place in obedience to God was righteous, but the purpose of His death is fulfilled only when men respond in faith and are thereby actually cleansed by His power and recreated in His holiness. *"[For without holiness] no man shall see the Lord"* (Heb. 12.14). Men stand therefore not merely in a position of holiness but are really made holy in Christ; and must remain so on the ground of their free agency and God's free grace. This is the only *perseverance* taught in the Bible! For, we stand or fall according to our response to His abundant grace provided in Christ's atoning sacrifice and work (Gen. 3.15; Rom. 5.8, 10-19). As Wesley said, His grace is *"free in all"* and *"free for all"*. In the same way, it is a false doctrine that purports that God eternally punishes all men for Adam's transgression; rather, a person is punished finally for his unbelief and actual rejection of Christ; just as a truly repentant believer is pardoned and cleansed by personally receiving Christ's transforming grace (Jn. 1.12; Rom. 12.2). Thus, we can never be justified by saying "the devil made me do it!" any more than Eve was justified in saying it. Every man is responsible for his own behavior, because God has provided the remedy for sin in Christ, and we all have access to His miraculous deliverance and have the freedom and power to choose (Rom. 6.15-23).

Wrong View of Imputation Breeds Lawlessness

We categorically reject, therefore, the traditional Calvinistic interpretation of *imputation*, not only because it is wrong on its face, but because it breeds lawlessness and substitutes in the place of Christ's transforming power the doctrines of man's inability to truly repent and turn from sin; to be recreated in His holiness; and to be kept by His grace in a state of true holiness.

No truths are plainer in the Bible than those which teach and demonstrate God's transforming power to instantly pardon and regenerate sinners, and subsequently to cleanse inbred sin instantly through a second divine work of grace----sanctification. Besides the biblical revelation that affirms the "first blessing" and the "second blessing", we have the universal witness of millions who have been transformed by God's power and have lived victorious sanctified lives! The key to such glorious liberty is to fully surrender to Christ every cherished idol and sin harbored in the heart, and willingly confess and commit oneself to forsake every known sin and to accept fully the lordship of Christ.

We heard of a Lutheran who witnessed to a Scotch-Irish Presbyterian on a certain occasion. He asked him if he believed the Bible to be God's Word. "I do", said he. "Well, do you sincerely believe Jesus is the Son of God, and that He died for all men" "I do", said he. "Do you believe this includes you." "I do." Then declared the Lutheran, "Then you are saved!" "Oh, no", said the sincere and enlightened Presbyterian: "for the same Bible that you have quoted also says, *'Let the wicked forsake his way, and the unrighteous man his thoughts: and let him return unto the Lord, and he will have mercy upon him . . ."* And then he concluded, "Since I'm not ready to forsake all to follow Christ, then I must disagree with you. For it's evident that I'm not really saved."

Such is the deficiency of Calvinism. It breeds lawlessness: for its proponents teach that the sins of believers---past, present, and future---have all been forgiven and punished on the Cross. While this could be construed in one sense to be true, it is not true in the sense that the Calvinist's means it: for it is purported that a sinner's habitual sinning is continuously covered by the blood of Christ once he is justified. The naïve victims of this false teaching thus not only anticipate their continual sinning but also their willing compliance with the *"spirit of disobedience"* is thereby justified. Under this delusion, some believers pray and ask forgiveness for the sins they are going to commit.

We heard of man some years ago who had received a speeding ticket from an officer and the next day paid the fine. Then on the following day he was again stopped for speeding by the same officer. The man showed the officer his receipt for the ticket he had received the previous day, hoping for pardon on the basis that the penalty he had already paid would be sufficient to cover the penalty for his present crime. Such is the rationale of Calvinism. It goes without saying that the officer and the court had a completely different view and interpretation of the incident.

Neither do believers under the impressions of Calvinism have to necessarily maintain a passionate worship and devotion to Christ to remain justified, for their perseverance is guaranteed by God's eternal decree: for the "elect" were predetermined to be saved before the foundation of world, or otherwise, as some other Calvinists teach, were predetermined to be saved after the fall of Adam in Eden. [40] Either way, some Calvinists even teach that justified believers are literally incorporated into Christ's glorified body in heaven, and thus they are perfectly secured though they may fall into gross sin! [41] In effect, God sees the personal

---

[40] The technical theological term *supralapsarianism* is used by Calvinists who hold the view that in the order of God's decrees, the election and reprobation of individual persons occurred before creation and the fall; whereas *infralapsarianism* or *sublapsarianism* is used by those who hold that God decreed to permit the fall of man into sin before decreeing to save some of humanity: the "elect". *Supralapsarianism* has been abandoned by almost all Calvinists in the past century or so.

[41] In refutation of these Calvinistic views, we recommend Henry E. Brockett, *Scriptural Freedom from* Sin (Nicholasville, KY: Schmul Publishing Co., 1980; Richard S. Taylor, *A Right Conception of Sin* [revised and enlarged edition] (Nicholasville, KY: Schmul Publishing Co., 2002; Randolph S. Foster,

righteousness of Christ in believers, though they may continue in a sinful state. Actual sins are thus nullified or rendered as nothing; for though a believer may backslide, yet he can "never finally fall away." Hence the saying, "Once in grace, always in grace!"

It was these errors that moved Jacob Arminius (1560-1609) and thereafter John Wesley, John Fletcher, Charles Finney and a great number of celebrated evangelical preachers to reject the basic premises on which Calvin had built his theological system---a system which he attempted to defend in his celebrated *Institutes of the Christian Religion*. Finney, after systematically dismantling Calvin's theological scheme, and exposing his errors with unsparing logic, wrote, "[For these reasons] I could never receive [Calvin's] theological fiction of imputation."[42]

It may be seen, upon carefully examining the Scriptures, that Jesus' righteousness is not imputed to man by a sovereign decree, but rather a man is justified by faith and his willingness to repent and be transformed in the image of Christ (Hab. 2.4; Rom. 1.17). Moreover, this call is universal and indiscriminate, not limited as hyper-Calvinists contend (2 Pet. 3.9; Rev. 22.17). In other words, faith is imputed **for righteousness**! So, *"Abraham believed God, and it was imputed unto him for righteousness"* (Jas. 2.23). Paul says in Rom. 4.3, *"it was counted unto him for righteousness,"* and then elaborates further, *"And therefore it was imputed to him for righteousness. Now it was not written for his sake alone . . . But for us also, to whom it shall be imputed, if we believe on him that raised Jesus from the dead"* (vv. 22, 23).

Objections to Calvinism As It Is (Nicholasville, KY: Schmul Publishing Co., 1998); and Wesley's *Calvinism Calmly Considered (loc. cit.)*.

[42] A.M. Hills, *Fundamental Christian Theology*, (Salem, OH: Schum Publishing Co., reprint 1980), p. 395.

In vv. 9-10, the word *"reckoned"* is used in the KJV, but the words *"imputed,"* *"counted,"* and *"reckoned"* are all translated from the same Greek word, *elogisthe*, and thus are synonymous in meaning: but *reckoned* seems to convey best the meaning of the original word. In any case, what is the *"it"* that was reckoned or imputed to Abraham for righteousness? Plainly, it was **his faith**. So, therefore, it is *faith* that is imputed for righteousness. It is not said that the righteousness of Christ is imputed to man, but rather the gift of faith is *"imputed for righteousness."* Or, it may be said, that righteousness is imputed through faith. In any case, God sees righteousness in faith, because once a soul conceives through faith and the Spirit and Word of God, and the new creature is born (Jn. 3.5-7; Jas. 1.21; 1 Pet. 1.23), there is empowerment for obedience to the law of God (Rom. 1.5; 6.1-2, 16; 16.26; 2 Cor. 10.5; Jas. 1.21-23; 2.17-26; 3.13). Therefore, faith and grace are no excuse for disobedience (Romans 6.1-2); rather these precious gifts from the Lord encourage and empower one to obey. Again, faith in the righteousness of Christ is no excuse for unrighteousness in men; rather a man is made righteous in Christ through faith.

Now observe; salvation is revealed in the Scriptures as something *imparted* to us by faith, not merely imputed (Rom. 5.5; 2 Cor. 1.22; 5.17; 8.16; Eph. 1.13; 4.30); therefore, we become *"partakers of the divine nature"* with the manifest proof of *"having escaped the corruption that is in the world"* (2 Pet. 1.4). A man does not, therefore, merely stand just before God, he is effectively made just; and, accordingly, he is not merely positioned as a saint, he is dynamically transformed into a saint! God does not merely see a man sanctified, He effectively sanctifies him!

On this same basis, we reject the doctrine that the sin of one man is imputed to another, particularly in the sense that it incurs eternal punishment: for the logical consequence of this view leads to pantheism and universalism: for if all are condemned because

92

of Adam's particular act of disobedience, and consequently inherited his particular guilt, then all must likewise automatically be justified in Christ and inherit His righteousness: for Adam and Christ are set over against each other as the representative heads of the human race (Rom. 5.12-14). Thus, accordingly, if all are damned for Adam's sin, then all must be saved by Christ's righteous act and "free gift." But what we see in the Scriptures is quite the contrary: men are finally saved and/or damned by their own personal choices, conditioned by their own personal faith in Christ or their doubt and defiance.

Calvinism therefore for obvious reasons must be rejected: for each man is saved by his faith and obedience or condemned for his lack of faith and disobedience (Hab. 2.4; Jn. 3.36; Rom. 1.16-17; 5.1; Gal. 3.11; Heb. 10.38). Thankfully, there are an ever-increasing number of scholars and teachers who now hold that imputation in Scripture never means the transference of one person's blessing or punishment to another. Albert Barnes, who was in his time a mild Calvinist, and an acclaimed biblical expositor and commentator, says in commenting on Rom. 4.3, that "The word [impute] is never used to denote charging one [for something] which does not properly belong to him." [43] We conclude, then, that while the whole race of man is reckoned depraved in Adam, still each man stands accountable finally for his own depravity and the sins he willfully commits. And each man must be willing to persevere in faith to realize his final salvation (Mt. 24.13; Mk. 13.13; 2 Pet. 1.10-11; Rev. 2.10-11): for every man chooses his own eternal destiny and is accountable for his own actions. So away with the errors of Calvinism!

---

[43] Hills, *Fundamental Christian Theology*, p. 394.

Infants Born in Sin

We have noticed that all men have received a depraved nature because of the fall of Adam, yet we are not punished for Adam's personal transgression, nor for the depravity passed on to us *per se*; rather we are finally punished for the sins we personally and willfully commit that spring from the depravity we inherited (Mt. 12.35-37; Rom. 14.12; Gal. 6.4-5; 1 Pet. 4.5). For *"every man"* will be judged finally *"according to his works"* (Rom. 2.6). It cannot be overemphasized that sin is in the final analysis a deeply personal matter (Gen. 20.4-6; Ps. 51.4; Lu. 15.21; Jas. 4.17); and, accordingly, each man is personally accountable for his sins and his separation from God (Rev. 20.11-13), which can only be if his actions spring from a free and conscious will.

We have stated therefore that sin is committed only in a conscious and deliberate act, at least in the sense that we are blameworthy and made finally accountable for it with eternal retribution. It is upon this basis that we hold that infants and small children are not accountable for their depraved nature, nor for their transgressions: for, strictly speaking, they are not capable of committing sin, that is, of consciously and defiantly rebelling against the expressed will of God: for they have not developed a moral consciousness (note the distinction made in Num. 15.28-30). In another sense, however, children were made sinners by Adam's fall (Rom. 5.12-14); yet, we know that they did not eat personally of *"the tree of knowledge of good and evil"*, for *"your little ones . . . [have] no knowledge between good and evil"* (Deut. 1.39; Is. 7.15-16; Rom. 9.11; et al), that is, infants and small children simply do not have carnal knowledge; and thus are not chargeable as such, neither for the depraved nature they inherit, nor for the actual "sins" they commit in ignorance or unintentionally (Lev.

4.1-3; 5.15-17; Num. 15.22-24; Ps. 19.12; et al). And, further, as we have shown elsewhere, the *free gift* of God's universal grace and the atoning sacrifice of Christ on the Cross, ordained before the foundation of the world, remitted the divine condemnation and eternal punishment of all men not directly responsible for the depravity they inherited (Lu. 12.47; Jn. 9.41; 15.22; Rom. 5.12-21; Jas. 4.17; Rev. 13.8). The foreordained shedding of the blood of Christ thus effectively reversed the judgment of God brought on by Adam (Gen. 6.8; 8.20-21; 9.7; Ps. 1.1-3; Rom. 5.12-21; Eph. 1.4-9).

Men do not become chargeable for sins and offenses until they arrive at what may be called the "age of accountability", when, like Adam and Eve, their *"eyes [are] opened"* to carnal knowledge (Gen. 3.1-11), a state of mind and consciousness that varies with each child depending on his unique personality traits and the peculiar social and religious factors that influence his life as he grows up. Then, after having become aware of the law of God and the consequences of his thoughts and actions, the morally conscious man or woman becomes fully accountable for his actions, and for the inherited state of depravity from which his actions spring.

It is unthinkable thus to hold to the old Augustinian-Calvinistic view that unbaptized infants are eternally damned. Under this delusion, it is reported that a Calvinistic preacher declared at a funeral of an unbaptized infant: "No doubt this infant is at this moment a writhing little viper in hell."[44] Sadly, this sentiment was espoused for centuries by believers throughout Europe; and similar things were said by both Roman Catholic and Protestant preachers in America in the sixteenth- through the twentieth centuries.

---

[44] Hills, *Fundamental Christian Theology*, p. 433.

It is unscriptural, and unlike God, we believe, therefore, to hold that infants and small children are chargeable for their parents' transgression in the Garden, and consequently deserving of eternal torment and divine retribution. A child is indeed subject to inherit a physical disease and the inclination to sin from his/her inherited depravity and God's universal curse upon the earth, but eternal condemnation and punishment are adjudged only upon a morally responsible person. All are judged finally for their deeds, not their depravity *per se.* This is borne out plainly in the Scriptures; thus, Paul admits that *"death reigned from Adam to Moses, even over them that had not sinned after the similitude of Adam's transgression"* (Rom. 5.14), which included infants and the mentally impaired. We may infer from passages such as Deut.1.39, Rom. 9.11, Mt. 18.3-6, 14, Mk. 10.14, that infants, though not held eternally accountable for decisions made by others, are nevertheless not spared physical death nor the unfortunate calamities that may befall them under the judgment of the universal curse---a condition that indiscriminately affects the just and unjust alike (Gen. 3.14-19; Rom. 8.18-23), a judgment that will continue to afflict men until it is lifted in the glorious age to come (Rev. 22.3).

Now we know that *"sin is not imputed where there is no law,"* and so Paul establishes his point that there must have been a moral law in force between the time of Adam and Moses: for death had reigned *"even over them"* that had not sinned in the way that Adam did. Therefore infants, being under the power of original sin through Adam, died physically and suffered the calamities that all men do under the penalty of God's curse; yet, being unable to sin, strictly speaking, like Adam had done in Eden (against the expressed commandment of God), they were reckoned blameless before the throne of God regarding any final retribution. In other words, the infant, like all men, will experience physical death

(Rom. 5.12; Heb. 9.27), and also pain and suffering, and the separation of soul and body because of death; yet the infant is not subject to the *"second death"* (Rev. 20.14), that is, the eternal separation of his soul from God: for the "second death" is applicable only to morally accountable men and women *"according to their works"* (Rev. 20.11-13). Paul's statement in Rom. 5.14 therefore does not contradict the fact that, before the revelation of Moses' law, those who consciously and willfully broke God's moral law---however that law was made known to them---were made accountable and liable to eternal punishment (Gen. 6.1-7; Jude 14-16).

Now observe; Deut.1.39 reveals the status of infants and small children before the Lord, which have *"no knowledge between good and evil."* They were permitted to enter the Promised Land, a type of heaven, for this very reason: because they had *"no knowledge between good and evil."* This would include of course all victims of abortion. Paul also in Rom. 9.11 indicates that children, having *"neither done any good or evil,"* are counted as part of God's elect. In Mt.18.3-6, 14, Jesus seems to equate children with innocence, humility, and the purity of His eternal kingdom.[45] In fact, he equates the new birth with the nature of children (v. 3). In v. 10 children are shown to have guardian angels, as do all of God's children (Ps. 34.7; 91.11; Heb. 1.13-14). Further, in v. 14, the principle that Jesus sets forth would seem to apply also to justification of children before God--- *"Even so it is not the will of*

---

[45] We will not cavil here over the distinction between "innocence" and unaccountability regarding infants. All are indeed born with depravity and, as such, with sinfulness, and thus on occasion manifest anger, greed, and other evil tempers. Infants are, thus, as Wesley argued, numbered among all men who need a Savior. But infants are also the recipients at birth of God's "preventing grace" provided through the atonement of Christ; and thereby their judgment and condemnation is removed, rendering them blameless and innocent (Wesley, *Works*, V, p. 647).

your heavenly Father which is in heaven, that one of these little ones should perish." Thus, though children are born in depravity, they are held accountable only for what they do after having developed a moral consciousness and thus are capable of sinning willfully; and only on that basis are they justly blamed for their actions. Until then, there is enough evidence in Scripture for us to hold that God, in consideration of Christ's atonement and universal grace, has included infants and young children among His elect, and thus had their names written in the Book of Life *"from the foundation of the world"* (Mt. 18.3-5, 10; 19.14; Rev. 3.5; 13.8; 17.8; 20.12, 15).

The love of God is greater far
Than tongue can ever tell;
It goes beyond the highest star,
And reaches to the lowest hell;
The guilty pair, bowed down with care,
God gave His Son to win;
His erring child He reconciled,
And pardoned from his sin
O love of God, how rich and pure!
How measureless and strong!
It shall forevermore endure,
The saints and angels' song.

Besides the Scriptural references just noticed, we have the historical account of David's concern for his child conceived illegitimately by Bathsheba (2 Sam. 12.13-23). The child was struck with a sickness from God and was decreed to die, due to the wickedness and adultery of David. Still, David fasted and cried unto the Lord for deliverance for the child, hoping He would change His mind. This was done apparently after David had repented for his great sin, the evidence of which may be seen in David's attitude of contrition and humiliation, and in his worship in the house of the Lord; but more explicitly it is shown in the decree of Nathan--- *"The Lord also has put away thy sin"* (v. 13). Now observe; though David's sin was forgiven, and he now stood clear before the Lord, the verdict of the Lord to take the child nevertheless stood, and the child died in infancy (v. 14). Yet David was assured that he would meet his infant son in heaven. His conclusion was, *"I shall go him, but he shall not return to me"* (v. 23). The child thus was born a bastard and suffered for seven days and died; yet he was not eternally accountable for his father's and mother's sin. The Lord indeed works in wondrous and mysterious ways---*"According as he has chosen us in him before the foundation of the world . . . having predestined us unto the adoption of children by Jesus Christ to himself according to the good pleasure of his will, to the praise of the glory of his grace, wherein he has made us accepted in the beloved"* (Eph. 1.4-6).

Therefore, we categorically reject the doctrines of certain Early Church bishops, like Cyprian (3rd century) and Augustine (5th century), who later influenced the Roman Catholic Church to consign all un-baptized infants to eternal damnation. And we reject with equal passion the theology of John Calvin in the 16th century, whose doctrines influenced his followers to teach that only certain infants are decreed by God to be saved, the rest (the great majority of them!) being foreordained to spend eternity in hell and damnation. Further, unlike these celebrated Christian leaders, we do not hold that the fate of infants is in a sacrament of baptism, or in a "God" who can eternally punish an infant for another's (Adam's) transgression. Baptismal regeneration has been justly called "water salvation," and is an absurd fiction of some religious traditions; it is certainly not a doctrine of the Holy Spirit that can find support in the Scriptures, and therefore it is not held by the ministers and members in Zion Assembly. Neither does the loving and just God of the Bible, contrary to what is taught by many Roman Catholic and Calvinistic teachers, punish infants arbitrarily with eternal torment, determined by a decree made before the world was created (Calvinism), or because someone or some religious institution has failed to baptize them---a doctrine that many Roman Catholic, Greek Orthodox, Lutheran, Anglican, and Presbyterian ministers have espoused and proclaimed. Rather, infants are covered by the atoning blood of Jesus until such a time that they are awakened to their sin and separation from God and are morally capable of rejecting Christ or of repenting and being reconciled to God.

Accordingly, in contrast to the harsh traditions of the men and religious traditions mentioned above, we hold that, though infants are born with depravity, no final punishment is consigned to them because of it; for eternal punishment without responsibility is a contradiction of moral reason, and a reproach to the goodness and justice of God. [46] No doubt this is one of the basic reasons that Jesus said of children, *"for of such is the kingdom of God"* (Mk. 10.14), by which He seems to allude to a certain blamelessness in them before God (v. 15). It is only reasonable to conclude that a child is accountable for his depraved nature, only when he becomes conscious and comprehensive of his sinfulness and can intelligently respond to the Holy Spirit's call to repentance and reconciliation to God. It is then that he makes the universal depravity his own. And this is supported fully in the Scriptures (Ps. 32.5; 51.3; 81.11; Prov. 1.22-31; Is. 1.18-20; Jer. 3.13; Hos. 5.15; Mk. 1.15; Jn. 1.12-13; 15.26; 16.7-15; Acts 13.48; Rom. 2.4; 10.8-17; 1 Cor. 1.26-28; 2 Cor. 7.9-10; Eph. 4.11-16; 1 Pet. 1.23; 2 Tim. 2.25; Titus 1.1; 1 Jn. 2.23, 29; Rev. 2.5, 21; et al.).

---

[46] Miley, *Systematic Theology*, II, 247-248.

So, whereas, all come into this world with a depraved nature, only those who consciously resist the convicting power of the Holy Spirit and God's call to repentance are eternally condemned and punished; and it should be borne in mind always that repentance is possible and necessary only when one has been made aware and becomes conscious of his sin, feels the weight of divine condemnation, and thus is capable of truly acknowledging his sin and turning intelligently and whole-heartedly to Christ. We are fully convinced that final reprobation is pronounced only upon a morally responsible person. Baptism is therefore not necessary to perform upon infants, but upon believers who have repented and have had their sins washed away by the Holy Spirit, and their consciences purged from guilt and dead works (Acts 24.16; Rom. 2.15; 13.5; Heb. 9.14; 10.22; 1 Pet. 3.16, 21).

Part 3

We have noticed that the original man and woman were created in the image of God (Gen. 1.26-27), and this image included intelligence/reason, will/self-determination, and affections/desires/passions). Adam and Eve were created holy, without sin, perfect. God breathed into man and he became a *living soul*---a self, a person, made in the image of God. His affections were pure; his will free and unencumbered and set positively to please the Lord. He not only had freedom of choice, he was free indeed (Gen. 2.16-17; Jn. 8.36). However, man's freedom---which included his power of choice and self-determination---opened the door for him to defy and rebel against God. The fact that man, through satanic temptation, chose to walk through this forbidden door resulted in what is called "the fall."

The Human Self and Sanctification

It is important to understand that when man fell in Eden, he did not fall from being human; each man thereafter remained a self, that is, each man retained the essential qualities of personhood. As such, man retained his intelligence, will, and affections, though these faculties were now damaged and disordered. Moreover, though the moral image of God in man was marred and distorted, his essential *self* continued to be, though now infected with carnality and inclined toward evil. This carnal nature, the "Adamic nature", rooted itself in man's heart and soul. Like a fungus, it permeated his entire being. Our missionary objective is not, therefore, to help rid men of their selves, but rather the corruption of their selves.

This point is important to understand; for in the divine work of sanctification, it is the corruption of the soul that is removed, not the self, the inner man. Grasping this truth enables one to avoid the errors of Romanism and Calvinism, on one hand, and the flood of vain imaginations and devilish doctrines now pouring into Christian thought from the East *via* Buddhism, Hinduism, Islam, and New Age religions. These religions either deny the self, as in Buddhism, or deny the remedy to remove the corruption of sin from the self through the Gospel of Jesus Christ, a denial that is maintained in Judaism, Hinduism, Islam, and, to their shame, the great majority of contemporary Christian sects and denominations.

Now observe; the Bible reveals plainly that it is the self that is renewed in regeneration and that is fully cleansed and restored in sanctification. We should be careful to maintain the distinction, therefore, between the self and the body of sin that has infected the self. The body of sin, the "old man," may be cut out of the self through the piercing two-edged sword of the Spirit, the Word of God which cuts away the corruption of *"the flesh"* (Eph. 5.26; 2 Thess. 2.13; 5.23; Heb. 4.12). This is what the prophet signifies by the *"circumcision of the heart"* (Jer. 4.4). He means the cutting away and casting out of the infectious, spiritual disease. Old Testament circumcision was thus a type of regeneration, not water baptism as many mistakenly assert. Thus, the apostle Paul: *"For he is not a Jew who is one outwardly, nor is circumcision that which is outward in the flesh; But he is a Jew which is one inwardly; and circumcision is that of the heart, in the Spirit, not in the letter . . . "* (Rom. 2.28-29). Christ is the Healer, the Restorer, the Deliverer, the Sanctifier! He now dwells in us through the dynamic power of the Holy Spirit. For anyone who will accept His gracious offer of sanctification by faith, He will cast out the *"old man,"* the corruption of the flesh that has infected the inner self (Gal. 4.22-30; Jn. 8.33-36). In Jesus' parable in Lu. 11.21-26, the cleansing of original depravity in the self must be included in His meaning of the *"strong man"* being cast out, and the house being *"swept and garnished":* for unless Christ and His Spirit indwell the house and make their abode there with the Father after cleansing (Jn. 14.23), there is nothing to prevent the evil of corruption or the "strong man" of returning and making the situation even worse than before (v. 26). This is perfectly in harmony with the apostle Peter's admonition and warning in 2 Pet. 2.20-22. It explains also Paul's mysterious language in Gal. 2.20: *"I am crucified with Christ: nevertheless, I live; yet not I, but Christ lives in me"*; and, again in Rom. 6.6: *"Knowing this, that our old man is crucified with him, that the body of sin might be destroyed, that henceforth we should not serve sin".* Here the apostle signifies that the self is now *"dead indeed unto sin, but alive to God through Christ"* (v. 11); it is freed from the entanglements and bondage of the flesh. The "inner man" has been born again and cleansed and restored in the image of God's holiness!

Still, however, man remains under the universal curse. This means that even sanctified men---men perfected in the image of God---must continue to resist the sin in the world. The physical aspects of man, his body and brain, remain after sanctification subject to the universal curse. In this state, even sanctified men must continue to *"cry out to be delivered"* from the infirmities connected with their physical bodies (Rom. 8.18-23). Accordingly, saints get sick, make mistakes in judgment, and finally physically die. So, while the saint no longer necessarily sins---for he desires only to please the Lord---yet the sin in the world, and the judgment of the universal curse, affect his physical frame and mental judgments. Our absolute perfection is thus not complete. There is still a glory to be attained (Phil. 3.8, 12-14; 2 Pet. 1.3-11; Jude 20-21). There is still a perfection in glorification. The sanctified believer must continue to move from *"glory to glory"* by the Spirit on his journey to Eternal Glory (2 Cor. 3.18).

Social Sin

We have emphasized that sin is a deeply personal matter. Notwithstanding, it is also expressed in corporate and collective acts. In fact, sin has infected the whole world, that is, all men are born alienated from God through the fall in Eden, and those who resist God's saving grace continue to be held captive to the influence and sway of Satan (1 Jn. 5.19). We live in a fallen world, a world that is hostile to God (Jn. 8.23; 12.25; 13.1; 16.11; 17.14; 1 Jn. 4.5). In addition to the effect of God's curse upon the world, Satan has succeeded to gain control over the world in general, bringing it under his deceptive influence and power. He rules men and their institutions and societies to one degree or another through demonic principalities and powers. And he strives to rule the church---to *"sit upon the mount of the congregation"* (Is. 14.13; Mt. 16.18-19; Eph. 6.10). Thus, though God is ultimately in control, Satan has been allowed to gather sinners together and to rule over a kingdom of evil. He is thus called the *"god of this world"* (2 Cor. 4.4), the *"prince of this world"* (Jn. 12.31), and the *"prince of the power of the air"* (Eph. 2.2).

Now, observe; we are admonished to abstain personally *"from the very appearance of evil,"* and not to be *"partakers in other men's sins"* (1 Tim. 5.22; Eph. 5.7). We are warned also against being drawn into unclean associations (2 Cor. 6.17; Rev. 18.4) and admonished not to run with the crowd (Ex. 23.2; Rom. 12.2). Thus, the psalmist, *"Blessed is the man that walks not in the counsel of the ungodly, nor stands in the way of sinners, nor sits in the seat of the scornful"* (Ps 1.1). Christians should be careful to *"walk circumspectly"* before God and to avoid worldly unions and evil associations, keeping themselves *"unspotted from the world"* (Jas. 1.27). Further, we are admonished to be sober and vigilant: for sin can find corporate expression in churches as well as in social and political institutions. Therefore, a Christian should use his status and influence as a churchman as well as a good citizen of the state to oppose and overturn evil in every quarter of government and society, but especially in the church. He should lift his voice to protest error and ungodliness in every form (1 Sam. 8.9; 2 Chron. 19.10; Ezek. 3.18, 19), and to separate himself from every agency and institution, secular or religious, that might cause him to conspire with others in corporate sin (2 Cor. 6.17; Rev. 18.4). If a Christian is privileged to live in a democratic nation, he should use his vote, as well as prayer, to make the society in which he lives compatible with, as much as possible, the will and purpose of God revealed in the Holy Scriptures (Rom. 13.1-7; 1 Tim. 2.1-3; Titus 3.1; 1 Pet. 2.13-17). In this way, the believer will not be blameworthy if the corporation, agency, or nation persists in indulging in evil (2 Chron. 19.10; Ezek. l 3.18-21; Acts 20.26-27).

"Deceivableness of Sin"

The apostle says in Rom. 7.11, *"For sin . . . deceived me,"* and in 2 Thess. 2.10 he refers to the *"deceivableness of unrighteousness."* This tells us that deception is at the very core of sin. Accordingly, when sin was *"found in [Lucifer],"* he became the great deceiver (Is. 14.12-14; Ezek. 28.15; 1 Jn. 3.8; Rev. 19.20; 20.10). Thus, it was sin that made him what he is! Satan is in fact a compulsive liar---the *"father of lies"* (Jn. 8.44). Sin and deceivableness therefore work together to destroy men.

For this same reason sinners endeavor to justify themselves: for they are deceived! And being deceived they go about deceiving others (2 Tim. 3.13; see also 2 Thess. 2.10; 2 Pet. 2.10-14; Jer. 17.9; 37.9). Moreover, all men endeavor, even as our first parents did, to conceal their sin, and like Satan and the serpent attempt to justify themselves by placing blame elsewhere (Gen. 3.14-18; Job 1.7-10; 2.1-5; 1 Jn. 3.8-10). It is only when we acknowledge our sin and truly repent that we can be saved and become disentangled from the deceptive power of sin. *"If we say we have not sinned, we make [God] a liar, and his word is not in us"* (1 Jn. 1.10).

But sin is also blinding and stupefying (Is 6.9, 10; Jn. 12.40; 1 Cor. 3.14; 2 Cor. 4.3-4). Observe; a corpse does not know the difference between the weight of a cotton ball and a five- hundred-pound anvil laid upon its chest, because it is dead. Neither do men who are *"dead in trespasses and sins"* feel the weight of sin; and, thus, they fancy themselves to be free. Their conscience is dull, and their eyes blind. They are like dumb oxen going to the slaughter, and birds hopping mindlessly to their snare, unaware that their very lives are about to be snuffed out (Prov. 4.22-23). Sinners thus run head long to their destruction and perish forever in the *"deceivableness of sin"* (2 Pet. 2.10-14).

The Scorpion and the Beaver

The tale of the scorpion and the beaver illustrates the deceptive nature of sin. The scorpion asked the beaver if he could ride his back across the river. "Do you think I'm crazy," said the beaver, "for, while I'm swimming, you'll sting me, and I'll drown." "Oh, come on," said the scorpion, sneering with laughter; "think for a minute . . . for if you drown, I would drown, too. So why would I sting you? It's not logical." The beaver pondered the scorpion's words, and said, "I see what you mean; that makes sense." So, the beaver said, "Hop on and off we'll go together." Then about half way across the river, the scorpion gave the gullible beaver a mighty sting. As they both were sinking to the bottom, the bewitched beaver anxiously asked, "Why did you do such a wicked thing? For even by your own logic, you knew we would both drown." The scorpion answered, "Logic has nothing to do with it, it's my nature; it's what I do."

It is thus that countless millions have been destroyed by the *"deceivableness of sin."* Even many Christians, having been once delivered from the quagmire of sin by the grace of God, have allowed themselves to be ensnared again by its deadly and seductive power; and many of these, finding no place for repentance, have perished in everlasting damnation. These deceived ones were allured away, *"through the lusts of the flesh, through much wantonness (sexual excesses), [having] clean escaped [those] who live in error"* (2 Pet. 2.18). And the apostle further adds, *"For if after they have escaped the pollutions of the world [through Christ], they are again entangled therein, and overcome, the latter end is worse than the beginning. For it had been better for them not to have known the way of righteousness, than after they had known it, to turn from the holy commandment delivered unto them. But it happened unto them according to the true proverb, the dog is turned to his own vomit again; and the sow that was washed to her wallowing in the mire"* (vv. 20-22).

There are indeed *"pleasures in sin for a season"* (Heb. 11.25), which the tempter, the wily one, magnifies to allure and attract his victims into his destructive trap. Recall the apostle's words in speaking about *"deceitful workers, transforming themselves"* to appear righteous before men. *"And no marvel; for Satan himself is transformed into an angel of light. Therefore, it is no great thing if his ministers also be transformed as the ministers of righteousness . . ."* (2 Cor. 11.14-15).

Sin works in mysterious ways; it is like *"the way of a serpent upon a rock"* (Prov. 30.19), difficult to trace and impossible to fully comprehend. It was the spirit of sin that first caught the attention of Eve, fascinating her with an almost hypnotic spell, under which she allowed herself to be entangled in a psychological web of delusion. She fell under the power of a lying spirit (Gen. 3.6; 2 Cor. 11.2). Finally, however, she was then drawn away by her own lusts, and God withdrew His life from her soul. She was now *"dead in sin"* (Rom. 5.12; 6.23; 1Tim. 5.6). Perhaps James, the Lord's brother, had the fall of Adam and Eve in mind when he drew his pattern of how sin works: *"But every man is tempted, when he is drawn away of his own lust, and enticed. Then when lust has conceived, it brings forth sin: and sin, when it is finished, brings forth death"* (Jas. 1.14-15).

How many, like Adam and Eve, have been deluded by the lying spirit of sin, and thereby go about attempting to justify themselves in their wickedness? The bars, brothels, and casinos, as well as many churches, are full of such persons. Under the delusions and deceitfulness sin, they endeavor to justify their corrupt addictions. Such are those who gamble away their tithes and offerings in casinos, and even ask God to bless their bets. Others are in bondage to tobacco habits, drugs and alcohol, and at the same time deny the devastating impact that these addictions are having on their lives. Millions are in bondage to various kinds of fornication and sexual lusts---pornography, fornication, homosexuality, adultery---and yet go to great lengths to cover their wickedness, even twisting and perverting the Word of God to justify themselves. Others, in the name of "love", burn in lust for one whom they call their "soulmate." They entangle themselves in adulterous marriages, covenanting with a second companion while the first is still living; and yet boldly attempt, under the powerful delusion of sin, to defend their sinful actions, among whom are countless preachers. They thus fulfill prophecy by calling *"evil good, and good evil, that put darkness for light, and light for darkness; that put bitter for sweet, and sweet for bitter!"* (Is. 5.20); and again, *"In transgressing and lying against the Lord, and departing from our God . . . and uttering from the heart words of falsehood"* (59.13).

Now observe; sin employs different methods to accomplish its destructive purposes. Sometimes horror and terror are used. It is well known that venomous serpents fix their piercing eyes upon their prey, until their victims are so full of amazement and terror that they are rendered incapable of escaping the serpent's advances. Under its spell-binding stare, birds have been known to drop from tree branches into their mouths as if paralyzed; rabbits and squirrels have been known to become so full of fear and confusion, that they have run right into the serpent's deadly grasp. On other occasions, however, sin camouflages itself, or works behind the scenes to snare its victims. *"Surely in vain the net is spread in the sight of any bird"* (Prov. 1.17): so, sin secretly sets its traps, to seduce and destroy the naïve and unwise.

Wealth, fame, and sexual pleasures have captivated the imaginations of many unsuspecting Christians, bringing them again into bondage, pulling some down so deeply under the power of sin that they never recover (Ec. 7.16; Hos. 13.9). How many have been seduced by the façade and flatteries of an adulterous woman (Prov. 6.24-29; 23.27, 28; 30.20), or by intoxicating wine when *"it is red, when it gives its color in the cup, when it moves itself aright"* (20.1; 23.31, 32; Is. 5.11; 28.1, 7), or the glitter of gold and desire for riches (1.10-19; 15.27; 21.6, 17, 26). Many prophets of God have fallen to these same deceptive enticements (Is. 56.10-12; 1 Tim. 6.11).

There is a fable connected with the lotus tree in North Africa, which says that if one eats of its fruit he will forget home. Sin has caused many a pilgrim to forget about his heavenly home, to go whoring after the things of this world, like the prodigal in Lu. 15.11-18. Faithful children of God, like Abraham, must therefore fix their eyes and hearts on the heavenly city (Heb. 11.8-10, 13-16), disciplining themselves to keep from turning to the left or the right: *"Let thine eyes look right on, and thine eyelids look straight before thee. Ponder the path of your feet, and let all your ways be established"* (Prov. 4.25-26). *"But ye, beloved, building up yourselves on your most holy faith, praying in the Holy Ghost, Keep yourselves in the love of God . . ."* (Jude 20-21).

Observe; because God does not always immediately punish the sinner, many are led to think that the Lord is *"slack concerning His promise"* (2 Pet. 3.9). This is another example of the *"deceivableness of sin."* It is said that if a cork is pressed down as much as a hundred feet deep in a lake and then released, it will rise again. But if it pressed down two hundred feet below the surface of the water, it will collapse and be destroyed because of the pressure. It is so with those deceived by sin. The greater the depth of sin, the less likely the sinner will ever be able to recover and be saved. *"Be not deceived; God is not mocked: for whatsoever a man sows, that shall he also reap"* (Gal. 6.7).

Delusion of Time

Another deceptive aspect of sin is in relation to time. The sinner is led to believe that he has plenty of time to prepare to meet God. How often we are warned in Scripture to avoid this fatal error; and rather to *"[redeem] the time, because the days are evil"* (Eph. 5.16; Col. 4.5). The Lord's brother, James, cautions against boasting about the future, for we *"know not what shall be on the morrow. For what is your life? It is even a vapor that appears for a little time, and then vanishes away"* (Jas. 4.14). There are many such warnings throughout Scripture (Job 7.7; Ps. 102.3; Jas. 1.10; 1 Pet. 1.24; 1 Jn. 2.17). But the most sobering warning comes from our Lord himself. In a parable in Lu. 12.16-20, Jesus tells about a man who was intensely engaged in a prosperous business, so much so that he took life for granted. He thus focused his attention on getting riches, giving no attention to the needs of his soul. He said to himself in arrogant self-confidence, *"Soul, thou hast much goods laid up for many years; take thine ease, eat, drink, and be merry"* (v. 19). But then suddenly came the thunderous judgment from the Lord, whom he had ignored, *"Thou fool, this night thy soul shall be required of thee . . ."* (v. 20).

It is a sobering thought that all of us are but flesh, finite and fragile; and as such, are merely one heartbeat away from death and eternity! The fact that death is indiscriminate is sobering; the infant, the young man, the strong, the mother with four children, the widow, the orphan, the rich, the poor, the famous, the corporate executive, the janitor, the social elite, the disenfranchised, the homeless, the saint, the ungodly, the free, the slave, all are subject to be killed or to drop dead at any given moment. It is foolish indeed to take life for granted, especially to waste away precious moments that God has so graciously given to us that we might answer Jesus' call to be saved: *"Come unto me, all you that labor and are heavy laden, and I will give you rest"* (Mt. 11.28; Mk. 8.34-38). *"He that believes on the Son has everlasting life: and he that believes not . . . shall not see life; but the wrath of God abides on him"* (Jn. 3.36).

It is an alarming and sobering reality that many Christians today are biblically illiterate. We may be sure that Satan is behind this modern-day trend; for the Holy Scriptures help us to see sin for what it is, and inspire us to overcome it (Rom. 3.20; 4.15; 5.20; 7.8-9). They make us *"wise unto salvation"* (2 Tim. 3.15). Lucifer knows this, and thus works in his bewitching fashion to prevent sinners from hearing the Word of God: for *"faith cometh by hearing, and hearing by the word of God"* (Rom. 10.17). At the same time, he works to hinder and prevent Christians from meditating in the Scriptures, and *"[studying] to show [ourselves] approved unto God"* (1 Tim. 4.13-61; 2 Tim. 2.15; see also Ps. 119.1-16, 24, 27, 30, 32, 34-36, 41, 45-48, 50, 52, 54, 59-63, 73-80, 88, 92-100, 104-105, 113-120, 130, 151-155, 160, 165, 172). Satan knows also that the Scriptures expose him and his tricky and deceptive ways (Mt. 4.1-11; Lu. 22.31; Jn. 12.31; 2 Cor. 4.3-6; 11.13-15; Gal. 1.6-9; 1 Pet. 5.8-9; Rev. 2.13; 12.3-12; see also Job 1.7; 2.2). Behold, how many have been *"taken captive by [Satan] at his will"* (2 Tim. 2.26).

Further, our adversary knows that the Holy Spirit empowers believers, and illuminates them to see the wisdom in the Bible that exposes the *"world, the flesh, and the devil"* (Jn. 16.7-15; 1 Cor. 2.1-5, 10, 13-16; Eph. 1.17-19). He thus schemes to weaken our faith and to hinder our prayer life: for he knows that faith and prayer, added to reading and meditation in the Word of God, will arm God's people with all the weapons needed to defeat him and destroy his influence (2 Cor. 4.4; Eph. 6.12-18; Jas. 4.7).

"Sin" and "Sins"

The Bible distinguishes between "sin" and "sins." On occasion, however, the word *sin* in some instances refers to all sins (Jn. 1.29, cp. with Is. 53.4-6, 11; 1 John 2.2) but in most cases to a specific sin (Mt. 18.15; Heb. 12.1). Thus sin is like the word, *corn*; it may refer to a single kernel, or to an ear of corn, or to a whole field of corn. The word is understood therefore in the context in which it is used. In many cases, the word *sin* refers to the body of sin, or the inherited nature of depravity, and is distinguished from actual sin, that is, the commission of an act of sin. The sin nature of man seems to be the primary significance in John the Baptist's proclamation of *"the sin"* in Jn. 1.29: *"Behold the Lamb of God, which taketh away the sin [not sins] of the world"*.

A classic passage that illustrates the distinction between *sin* and *sins* is 1 Jn. 1.7-9. The *"sins"* in v. 9 are transgressions acted out by the sinner---*acts* of unrighteousness---whereas the *"sin"* in vv. 7-8 is the *state* of unrighteousness, that is, original sin, native depravity. It was the realization of this state of unrighteousness that prompted the apostle Paul to acknowledge the *"sin which dwelleth in me"* (Rom. 7.17), and to recognize it as a tyrannical monarch: *"sin reigned in death"* (5.21). Sin must therefore be a state of being (native depravity or original sin), not merely a momentary and single act of the will.

Observe; sin is the *ground* of sins; the spirit and basis of lawlessness (1 Jn. 3.4); "the reign of an evil principle that works out of the sinner in acts of unrighteousness. Thus Paul: *"But I see another law in my members, warring against the law of my mind, and bringing me into captivity to the law of sin which is in my members"* (Rom. 7.23). *Sin* is the root of the tree; sins are the fruit the tree bears. *Sins* cause guilt and the need to be forgiven; *sin* is inward corruption that must be cleansed, eradicated---the hostile power that exists in the heart from which one must be delivered and freed! *Sin* is character, *sins* are conduct. *Sin* the producer, *sins* the product. *Sin* is what we are born into, *sins* are what we do. *Sin* is the want of righteousness, *sins* are unrighteous deeds. *Sin* is the sun, *sins* the planets orbiting the sun. [47] Thus, Jesus says, *"Whosoever commits sin [the implication here is 'he who keeps on sinning'], is the servant of sin"* (Jn. 8.34), that is, *the sin*, the "old man," must be eradicated for the believer to be made free (v. 36). It is difficult indeed for the motions of *sins* to cease, while *the sin* remains!

"Kill the Spider"

We are reminded of the deacon in a denominational church who was known to be rather carnal, and yet allowed to conduct prayer meetings on a regular basis. Since his sins were public knowledge, his prayerful conclusion at each meeting---"O Lord, clean all the cobwebs out of my life!" tended to annoy and insult the sincere members of the church. Finally, a little lady in the congregation could stand it no longer. In the next meeting, when the old deacon ended his prayer in the usual manner, she jumped to her feet and shouted, "Forget the cobwebs, Lord. Kill the spider!"

It has been pointed out that inbred sin is racial, or racially connected, that is, transmitted and passed on in humans by natural generation. We have emphasized, however, that we are not accountable for Adam's personal sin, but for the sinful nature inherited from him, which disposes us to commit our own sins. This fallen nature in man is plainly revealed in the Scriptures, but

---

[47] Strong, *Systematic Theology*, pp. 549-560.

also in the universal experience of humankind.[48] Plato wrote that there is "in all of us…a lawless wild beast nature." Immanuel Kant spoke of the "radical evil" in humans, and Sigmund Freud of the "unclean and evil beasts in the subconscious mind."[49] It is this radical evil deeply seated in man's moral nature that only the power of God through *"sanctification of the Spirit"* can eradicate (Rom. 6.6-7; Gal. 2.20; 2 Thess. 2.13). Simple pardon of acts of transgression will not free us from the "evil beast within" that disposes us to commit outward acts of transgression.

Be of sin the double cure,
Save from wrath and make me pure

The Good News is that both sin and sins have their cure in the same Source---the grace of God through faith in the shed blood of Christ. But this cure is actualized in two divine works: in regeneration (forgiveness and renewal) and sanctification (eradication and perfection). Sanctification perfects regeneration, that is, brings the believer to the point of a second crisis experience which enables him to deal with and crucify inbred sin. In this wonderful and glorious transformation, the "old man," the "body of sin," is crucified and destroyed. The believer is thus freed from the shackles of sin and becomes a joyful and unencumbered servant of Christ (Jn. 8.36; Rom. 6.6-7, 14). Glory to His name!

---

[48] Even the celebrated Augustus H. Strong, a moderate Calvinist, was forced to admit this in agreement with the esteemed E. G. Robinson who was fond of saying, "imputed righteousness and imputed sin are as absurd as any notion that ever took possession of human nature" (Strong, *Systematic Theology*, p. 594).

[49] Strong, *Systematic Theology*, pp. 549-596.

"Sin not unto Death . . . Sin unto Death"

In 1 Jn. 5.16-17 we have the apostle's strange-sounding language about *"sin not unto death"* and *"sin unto death."* The meaning of these verses has been vigorously debated through the centuries. In answer to this difficult passage, we respond, *First*, the Roman Catholic distinction between so-called "venial sins" and "mortal sins" should be ruled out as a viable interpretation of this passage; for these doctrines distort the biblical view of sin, making some sins seem unimportant, and holding that lesser sins do not break a right relationship or a justified standing with God. Thus, accordingly, mortal sins---murder, adultery, e.g.---are serious and therefore "unto death," and venial sins are "slight" and therefore "not unto death." While it is true that some sins are weightier and more damaging than others, still all sins war against the Spirit of God and are transgressions of His law and commandments. The Roman Catholic doctrine of "venial sins" and "mortal sins" are therefore obviously merely theoretical and the "commandment of men", and, as such, must be rejected by God's church: for any sin, if it is not removed through repentance and faith, will be finally "unto death" (Rev. 21.27; 22.14-15). *Second*, some hold to the view that these verses apply to civil laws and the judgments of civil courts and governments, which condemn criminals of capital crimes *"unto death,"* and sentence criminals of lesser crimes to punishment but *"not unto death."* Accordingly, there is no use to intercede in the case of capital crimes, for the law is fixed and unforgiving; whereas, there is hope for less severe cases, in which the believer might intervene to get the person's sentence reduced, and to pray for the accused to be spiritually restored. This interpretation has some merit for consideration, but it cannot possibly be made to square with John's meaning in this place; for, first, the church is the superior judge of sin, not civil courts and governments; and, second, the apostle's overall concerns throughout the entire book of 1 John are focused on relations within the church between God and the members, and the members with one of another in perspective of perfect love.

John Wesley interpreted these verses in a similar way to the notion just mentioned, only from a perspective within the context of the church, rather than civil courts. He understood the meaning of "death" in these verses to be physical death; so therefore, there is a sin unto physical death, and a sin not unto physical death. He understood Jas. 5.14-15 in this light, and thus interpreted the verses in John to mean that God punishes some believers for their sins with sickness, and, among these, for whatever reasons He has determined that some should die for their sins. This view seems consistent also with the apostle Paul's observation in 1 Cor. 11.27-30; see also Jer. 7.15-16; Prov. 1.24-32; Heb. 6.4-8). In these cases, there is no need to pray for deliverance, for God has decreed the sentence of death. This does mean, according to Wesley, that the person cannot be saved; in fact, some are saved because of the Lord's chastisement with sickness, even to death. [50] Wesley testified that he knew of many such cases, and that among these some confessed that death was a just sentence for them. In any case, the Lord made the determination, according to the counsel of His infinite wisdom, that some should die because of their sin. While Wesley's view may sound strange, it nevertheless has much support in the Scriptures. To his credit, Wesley admitted that this may not be only meaning of the verses.

Related to Wesley's view are instances throughout the Bible of men and women who died physical deaths for certain sins. Some

---

[50] *Wesley's New Testament: Translation and Notes in Modern English:* II, pp. 554-555, 587.

died physically in the New Testament for abusing the Lord's Supper, of which mention has already been made (1 Cor. 11.30). There is the case of David's bastard son, whom God took in death because of David's and Bathsheba's sin (2 Sam. 12.9-18); and though David was forgiven of his sin, the Lord nevertheless took the child because of it. In this case, there was no use to intercede to reverse the decision---as David had tried---for the divine decree was made. There is the case of Uzziah who was struck down by the Lord for touching the Ark of the covenant against the divine commandment (2 Sam. 6.3-7). No intervention was made in this case, though David would have been glad if it were possible. Then there is the case of the daughter of Jephthah who died because of her father's rash vow (Judg. 11.30-31, 35-40); though she seems to have been a good and proper child, and Jephthah himself otherwise a good man and hero of faith (Heb. 11.32). There is also the strange account of the nameless prophet from Judah in 1 Kg. 13.1-32, who, though he was mightily used by the Lord, yet did not heed carefully to the commands of God, allowing himself to be deceived by the false prophet from Bethel---a prophet similar in many respects to the infamous Balaam---and consequently was destroyed by a lion. The mighty hand of Providence had intervened, and the man of God from Judah suffered death for his disobedience. We have the case in the New Testament church of Ananias and Sapphira, who lied to the Holy Ghost and to Peter, and consequently dropped dead at the feet of the apostle for their conspiracy and sin (Acts 5.1-10).

There are many other instances that could be cited in the Sacred Book to illustrate that some sins are divinely ordained "unto death." It is indeed, *a fearful thing to fall into the hands of the living God!* Certainly, what Wesley has written in this regard cannot be contradicted, but, still, it remains open to argument if the apostle had Wesley's view of physical death in mind in the passage under consideration. Wesley himself admitted, as already noted, that this view was only one possible meaning of the term *"sin unto death."*

Thankfully, the language the apostle uses in these verses is probably stranger to our ears than the meaning. One of the first rules of biblical interpretation is that the most obvious meaning of a passage is likely the correct view, and thus a passage should be examined first with this in mind. However, a second rule says that, as biblical interpreters and teachers, we should *"study to show ourselves approved unto God"* (1 Tim. 2.15); for the meaning of some passages is deeper than our mind's first impressions. Our aim should always be to know the mind of Christ, and this requires consecration in the Spirit, and the discipline of "thinking through" certain passages prayerfully to get "the mind of Christ" (1 Cor. 2.16; Rom. 8.26-27). A third rule in biblical interpretation is that any verse or passage of Scripture should be judged in the context of the entire chapter in which it is written, and even in the context of the entire book; in fact, we should seek to understand every verse and passage in the context of the whole Bible (2 Tim. 2.15; 2 Pet. 1.19-21); for as the old schoolmen used to say, **Sacra scriptura sui interpres**, "Holy Scripture interprets itself." We will endeavor therefore to apply these methods here to understand the apostle's meanings in this passage.

Accordingly, since all sin leads to death, spiritually and physically (Gen. 2.16; Rom. 5.21; 6.21; Jas. 1.5), the apostle seems to signify by the term, *"sin not unto death,"* to a sin that is removed through repentance, faith, and regeneration, which produces new life in Christ. The term seems to be in reference therefore, at least primarily, to spiritual death: for only the sentence of spiritual death is removed when one is pardoned, the universal curse of physical death remains for saint and sinner alike. *"It is appointed unto men [all men] once to die"* (Heb. 9.27; see also Gen. 3.19; Eccl. 3.20).

Indeed, the *"sting of death"* (physical death) is the saint's *"last enemy"* (1 Cor. 15.26). The judgment of physical death against believers is removed only in the Rapture and glorification of the saints---the first resurrection (Rom. 8.18-23; 1 Cor. 15.51-55; 1 Thess. 4.16-18). Then will be fulfilled the inspired saying, *"Death is swallowed up in victory."*

John's term, *"sin not unto death"* thus seems to signify any sin for which the believer repents and is forgiven, and which the Lord graciously washes away. To His praise and glory, the Lord is gracious and merciful and ready to forgive. Obviously, if the Lord forgives and washes away our sin, it is *"not unto death"* (spiritual death): for our sin is removed from us *"as far as the east is from the west"* (Ps. 103.12), and our life in Christ and communion with the Father is restored; nor does it seem to apply to physical death: for physical death is a sentence pronounced upon the whole race of man because of original sin. This seems to be supported further by the apostle's admonition for us to intercede for a brother who may sin (v. 16), so that the offense might be removed, and that it not be "unto death" (spiritual death). Moreover, the sin in this case must be actual and outward, for *"if any man **sees** his brother sin."* These words seem to parallel Jesus' words in Mt. 18.15-20. In both cases, we are encouraged to make intercession for a brother who sins, to restore him to life in Christ and fellowship with the Father and the church. The weight of evidence thus seems to come down on the side of spiritual death and spiritual life as the primary meaning of the apostle in this place, though it does not exclude necessarily a more distant reference to physical death.

In v. 18 of this same passage, John says that *"whosoever is born of God sins not, but he that is begotten of God keeps himself, and that the wicked one touches him not."* The word "sin" here is a verb used in the present active indicative tense, which means the born-again believer has ceased to sin; he no longer continues in sin, that is, "he does not keep on sinning." Since there is no such thing as "sinless perfection," this verse cannot mean that the believer cannot sin. In fact, we know all too well, both by examples in Scripture and by experience, that a believer may stumble or slip into sin. Accordingly, we are told *"if"* [not when] any man sin, we have *"an advocate with the Father, Jesus Christ the righteous"* (1 Jn. 2.1). Jesus encouraged us also to intercede for any brother who sins, and to seek for his deliverance and reconciliation (Mt. 18.15-20). The apostles also have given us many instructions along these lines (Rom. 15.1-3; Gal. 6.1-2; Heb. 12.12-13; Jas. 5.19-20).

The term *"sin unto death"* is a little more difficult to grasp, because of the apostle's further comment: that we should not intercede in behalf of the person under the sentence of it. Some of the early church fathers, like Tertullian (A.D. 160-220), thought this term applied to apostates and counterfeits, because their blasphemies and apostasies had dulled them to the point that they could not sincerely repent; thus, the judgment of death, spiritual and physical, had already been made final. Tertullian interpreted Heb. 6.4-6, 8 in this way and applied it to John's meaning in the verses under consideration. These terrifying verses seem also to parallel with Heb. 10.26-31. We believe of course that a person can become so phony in his thoughts and affections, so that his conscience becomes "seared" rendering him unable to sincerely repent and be reconciled to God (1 Tim. 4.2; Eph. 4.17-19; Rom. 1.21; 1 Thess. 4.6-8). If this be the case, we do no injury by connecting these passages with Jesus' term, *"blasphemy against the Holy Ghost,"* and His teaching about unforgivable sin (Mt. 12.31-37), which has been considered already in Part II. Is John merely re-phrasing Jesus' words here a little differently? This is not out of the realm of possibility; but we admit a perfect understanding of the passage is difficult to grasp and comprehend.

Certainly, it is possible that there is more than one nuance of meaning in the apostle's words in John 5.16-17. We should not be surprised therefore if his words---having been written under the inspiration of the Spirit---includes all of the nuances of meaning mentioned above, except for the Roman Catholic view that tends to excuse and minimize in popular thought and practice the seriousness and consequences of so-called "venial sins" (i.e., "little sins"). Recall in Song of Solomon 2.15 that it is the "little foxes" that spoil the vines, which is almost certainly a reference to guard against any romantic inclinations that might lead to pre-marital sex.

Wesley's view of the text now under consideration has much to commend it, though we see no reason to limit death to its physical meaning. But neither did Wesley. In any case, there is no contradiction between our interpretation and Wesley's, and, in fact, we agree wholly with him in the sense that believers should consider sin with utmost gravity and profound seriousness, for we all must finally give an account for our behavior in this life: for either the glory of eternal life in heaven or everlasting damnation in hell await each of us! *And death and hell were cast into the lake of fire"* (Rev. 20.14).

Punishment for Sin

Death is not natural, at least not in view of God's original plan and purpose (Gen. 3.3-4; Rom. 5.12-14). Had it not been for sin, man would have lived forever in his natural body. Physical as well as spiritual death is the result of sin. Salvation immediately removes the penalty of spiritual death; and the first resurrection removes the penalty of physical death. In Christ, men have eternal life, first spiritually in this world, then in glorification in the world to come.

Now observe; everlasting death and damnation is the ultimate penalty that God justly imposes upon the unrepentant sinner (Gen. 2.17; Rom. 6.23; 1 Cor. 3.17; Rev. 21.8). The severity of divine punishment and retribution reveals how God himself sees sin. To Him, it is a loathsome and despicable disease in the soul of man; it is the spirit of rebellion and disobedience that separates Him from His creation. A holy God cannot live in fellowship with the sinner. Sin is His enemy! (Ps. 94.20; Amos 3.3; Jn. 8.31-47; 17.10-26; 2 Cor. 6.14-18; Jas. 4.4; 1 Jn. 1.6; 2.15). Its dominion must be conquered and destroyed! *"For sin shall not have dominion over you"* (Rom. 6.14). *"Let not sin therefore reign on your mortal body . . ."* (v. 12). Therefore, if the sinner clings to his sin, he cannot have fellowship with God. Eternal separation from God, *"the second death"* is thus the fitting sentence for the sinner who refuses to accept by faith God's remedy for his sinfulness in Christ, who desires to deliver and sanctify all who call upon Him in faith and sincerity (1 Thess. 4.3; 5.23; Heb. 10.10; Rev. 20.12-15).

There are consequences for sin also in this present world. It is often punished here and now. Throughout the Bible there are hundreds of instances that show that God punishes people for sinning. God has ordained civil government and discipline to punish evil doers (Ex. 21.23-24; Rom. 13.1-7; Titus 3.1; 1 Pet. 2.14), but often He also intervenes directly. Instances of divine interventions are replete throughout the Scriptures. But let the case of the Adam and Eve in Eden suffice here: for through their sin the whole world has since felt the *"sting of death"* and has endured pain and suffering (Gen. 3.14-19).

There are at least three basic reasons the Lord punishes sin. *First,* it is a deterrent. Punishment discourages men from sinning, and helps them to dwell together socially, without which there could be no civilization. God has thus ordained temporal *"punishment of evildoers"* (1 Pet. 2.14), as well as *chastisement* for the righteous (Heb. 12.7-11). *Second*, punishment is therapeutic; it is for reforming purposes. God chastises His own people, to transform and purify and perfect them in His image (Job 5.17; Ps. 92.12; Is. 26.16; 2 Cor. 6.9; Heb. 12.5-11; Rev. 3.19). He has even used wicked nations and men to punish His people to bring about their restoration and perfection (Hab. 1.2-4; 2.1, 4-20). The Lord also punishes sinners, here and now, to improve their character, both for their own good and for the good of God's people who live among them. God's people are thus admonished to pray for civil government and rulers, for they are *"the [ministers] of God for you for good"*, so that we might be able to live *"quite and peaceable [lives]"* (Rom. 13.4). *Third*, God punishes sinners forever in the lake of fire, because it is consistent with His eternal law and justice. He upholds and enforces His law. Eternal punishment is therefore God's righteousness at work. His *wrath* is a divine perfection, an attribute of His holy character: a perfection deserving of our praise, certainly not something for which the church should apologize. To be consistent with His own nature of holiness and justice, He must necessarily cast away the sinner finally and forever from His presence (Mt. 25.41; 2 Thess. 1.8-9; Rev. 14.10-11; 20.11-15).

Remedy for Sin

The Good News is that the shedding of Jesus' blood has provided the remedy for sin, the means for reconciliation with a holy God (Rom. 5.15-19; Heb. 9.22). Through grace, and sanctifying faith in Christ, transgressions are forgiven and the "old man," the sin nature, is crucified and purged. So, just as *in Adam* all die, so *in Christ* all may be quickened to newness of life and wholly sanctified (Rom. 6.4-6, 9-13, 22; 1 Cor. 15.22; 1 Thess. 5.23). The fall and the curse are reversed in Christ. Behold the wisdom and glory of God! The Father is reunited through regeneration and sanctification with His estranged creation.[51]

> *Sinners Jesus will receive;*
> *Sound this word of grace to all*
> *Make the message clear and plain;*
> *Christ receiveth sinful men.*

In *justification* and *regeneration*, actual transgressions are pardoned and washed away and a babe in Christ is born (Rom. 3.28-30; 5.1; Eph. 2.5, 13-18; Heb. 5.12-13; 1 Pet. 2.2); yet the "body of sin," the very nature of sin rooted in man's heart remains. In *sanctification*, this deeper level of sin is uprooted and removed (Rom. 6.6; Galatians 2.20; 5.23; 6.14; Col. 3.3-10); the "body of sin" is purged, and the sanctified believer is made free from sin (Jn. 8.36; Rom. 6.7; 1 Pet. 4.1). But observe; when a person is justified and regenerated, and his actual sins are washed away, a mighty battle immediately ensues between the "new man" and the "old man" (Rom. 6.6, 12-16; Eph. 4.22-24; Col. 3.1-10). It is as if the "old man" [original sin, the sin nature] launches a great campaign to hold on to his place in the new-born babe in Christ. Accordingly, the new convert must wrestle and fight, like the apostle himself did (Rom. 7.23-24), and the patriarch Jacob before him (Gen. 32.24-28), till the power of Christ crucifies the *"old man with his deeds"* (Rom. 6.6; Gal. 5.24; 6.14; Eph. 4.24; Col. 3.9).

Behold how many have been torn apart, spiritually and psychologically, by the allurements of sin, on one hand, and their

---

[51] Wesley, *Works*, VI, pp.234-240.

consciences on the other. Every new Christian, genuinely born again, quickly discovers, somewhat like Dr. Jekyll in Robert Louis Stephenson's classic tale---*Dr. Jekyll and Mr. Hyde*---that there is an evil Mr. Hyde seeking preeminence in his life. The new believer is the ground upon which two warring natures---God's Spirit and the flesh (Rom. 6.16-22; 7.23-25; 8.5-7; Gal. 5.17) fiercely engage in mortal combat, each fighting to conquer the believer's inner self, his soul, and to establish his throne there.

The war between the flesh and the Spirit of God is declared at the very moment the believer claims Christ as his Savior and is truly regenerated. The "old man" immediately answers, "But I shall not die, and in fact I will re-conquer what I have lost. I will reclaim this soul for myself!" At that point in the believer's life, he will do one of three things: *1*) go on to seek and cry out to God to be wholly sanctified until the victory is won, and he is made free from sin (Jn. 8.36; Rom. 6.17-22); *2*) deny to Christ the glory and power and desire to instantly and definitively sanctify him, and thus to accept the civil war going on inside of him as an inevitable and perpetual state of being in this life: and to adopt a lifestyle in which he resigns himself to constantly seek for forgiveness and reconciliation with God and man for transgressions committed; *3*) completely apostatize and live a totally defeated life, even if he continues to profess salvation.

In his 1913 book, *The Last Great Conflict*, A. J. Tomlinson gives a classic description of the second work of grace in his personal experience. We quote here at length his inspirational account:

> "Some little time after (I got saved), I fell into a tremendous conflict with an "old man" who gave me a violent contest. I fought him and wrestled with him day and night for several months. How to conquer him I did

not know. Nobody could tell me or give me encouragement. I had some serious thoughts of building a little booth out in the middle of a certain field, where I could be alone with God and the Bible . . . I was making a corn crop, and I suppose I prayed in nearly every row, and nearly all over the field. Though I worked hard every day, I frequently ate but one meal a day. I remember it as if it were but yesterday. I would leave the house at night at times and stay out and pray for hours. I searched my Bible and prayed many nights till midnight and two o'clock, and then out at work again next morning by sun up. It was a hard fight, but I was determined for that "old man" to die. He had already given me much trouble, and I knew he would continue to do so if he was not slain. I saw it, and I knew he must be destroyed or I would be ruined, and my soul dragged down to hell by his subtile [*sic*] influence and cruel grasp.

"At last the final struggle came. It was a hand to hand fight, and the demons of hell seemed to be mustering their forces, and their ghastly forms and furious yells would no doubt have been too much for me had not the Lord of heaven sent a host of angels to assist me in that terrible hour of peril. But it was the last great conflict, and I managed, by some peculiar dexterity, to put the sword into him up to the hilt.

"It was about twelve o'clock in the day. I cried out in the bitterness of my soul: 'Now! Now! You've got to give it up now! Now!' I felt him begin to weaken and quiver. I kept the 'Sword' right in him, and never let go. That sharp two-edged 'Sword' was doing its deadly work. I did not pity him. I showed him no quarters. There we were in that attitude when all of a sudden came from above, like a thunderbolt from the skies, a sensational power that ended the conflict, and there lay the 'old man' dead at my feet, and I was free from his grasp."

"Sinning Christians?"

The passages cited below are but a few of literally hundreds in the Bible that could be noticed to show the untenable position of those who support and promote the idea of "sinning Christians", that is, the doctrine that asserts that not even truly *"born again"* believers can cease from committing willful sin. Many who support this view admit that habitual sinning is condemned in the Word of God: but they deny that saints can cease from sinning altogether. When pressed, they usually confess their deep-seated belief that Christians are bound to sin more or less every day.

The unavoidable result of this theological perspective is that it denies or diminishes to a more or lesser degree the efficacy of Jesus' sufferings, death, and resurrection, and the power of His sanctifying grace. The advocates for sin ignore the fact that *"For this purpose the Son of God was manifested, that he might destroy the works of the devil"*, and that Christ is able to *"take away our sins . . . crucify our old man . . . keep [us] from falling, and to present [us] faultless [blameless] before the presence of His glory with exceeding joy"*.

Examine carefully the following passages:

> *"Afterwards Jesus . . . said unto him, Behold, thou art made whole: sin no more, lest a worse thing come unto thee"* (Jn. 5.14 KJV). The NIV has *"stop sinning"* for the

KJV phrase *"sin no more"*. The NASV has *"do not sin anymore."*

"Jesus said unto her, Neither do I condemn thee: go, and sin no more" (Jn. 8.11). The NIV has *"Go now and leave your life of sin"*. The NASV has *"From now on sin no more."* The verb here, as in the case in Jn. 5.14, is in the aorist tense in the original Greek text and denotes not simply to cease to commit habitual sin but to stop sinning altogether.

"For even hereunto were ye called . . . that we should follow in [Jesus'] steps: Who did no sin, neither was guile found in his mouth . . . Who his own self bare our sins in his own body on the tree, that we, being dead to sins, should live unto righteousness" (1 Pet. 2.21-24).

"Forasmuch then as Christ hath suffered in the flesh, arm yourselves likewise with the same mind: for he that hath suffered in the flesh hath ceased from sin" (1 Pet. 4.1). Again, the sense here is "has stop sinning."

"What shall we say then? Shall we continue in sin that grace may abound? God forbid. How shall we that are dead to sin, live any longer therein? . . . For he that is dead is freed from sin . . . Let not sin therefore reign in your mortal body, that ye should obey it in the lusts thereof. Neither yield your members as instruments of unrighteousness unto sin . . . Know ye not, that to whom ye yield yourselves servants to obey, his servants ye are to whom ye obey; whether of sin unto death, or of obedience unto righteousness? But God be thanked, that ye were the servants of sin, but ye have obeyed from the heart that form of doctrine which was delivered you.

Being then made free from sin, ye became the servants of righteousness" (Rom. 6.1-2, 7, 12-13, 16-18).

"My little children these things write I unto you, that ye sin not. And if any man sin, we have an advocate with the Father, Jesus Christ the righteous . . . And hereby we do know that we know him, if we keep his commandments. He that saith, I know him, and keepeth not his commandments, is a liar, and the truth is not in him. But whoso keepeth his word, in him verily is the love of God perfected: hereby know we that we are in him. He that saith he abideth in him ought himself also to walk, even as he walked" (1 Jn. 2.1-6).

"Whosoever abideth in him sinneth not: whosoever sinneth hath not seen him, neither know him. Little children let no man deceive you: he that doeth righteousness is righteous, even as he is righteous. He that comitteth sin is of the devil; for the devil sinneth from the beginning. For this purpose the Son of God was manifested, that he might destroy the works of the devil. Whosoever is born of God doth not commit sin; for his seed remaineth in him: and he cannot sin, because he is born of God" (I Jn. 3.6-9).

"But ye, beloved, building up yourselves on your most holy faith, praying in the Holy Ghost, Keep yourselves in the love of God . . . hating even the garment spotted by the flesh. Now unto him that is able to keep you from falling, and to present you faultless before the presence of his glory with exceeding joy, To the only wise God our Savior, be glory and majesty, dominion and power, both now and ever. Amen" (Jude 20-25).

In view of the many explicit commands and admonitions by our Lord and His apostles for believers to stop sinning, it is mind-boggling that so many Christian ministers and professing believers, indeed the great majority of them, continue to teach otherwise, asserting that in this present world there is no cure against this malady of the fallen human condition. They argue desperately to convince Christians that there is no full cure for sin in this present life, and thus that Christians must continue to sin. As if under a spell, they seem compelled by the very power they are unwittingly defending to boldly contradict Jesus' and the apostles' teachings and admonitions on the subject; and in the process also deny, either explicitly or implicitly, that the shed blood of Christ is a sufficient cure for all sinfulness, innate and actual, and that the Holy Spirit can keep believers in a state of sanctified grace.

Calvinists and other advocates for sin readily point to 1 Jn. 1.8, 10 to support their view: *"If we say we have no sin, we deceive ourselves, and the truth is not in us . . . If we say that we have not sinned, we make him a liar, and his word is not in us"*. The apostle here may have anticipated the Pelagian heresy in the fourth century which denied original sin and its consequences. But, in any case, he is pointing out that to be redeemed one must first confess the sins that he has committed and humbly acknowledge his need for forgiveness. This is made plain is v. 9 sandwiched between the verses just quoted: *"If we confess our sins, he is faithful and just to forgive us our sins, and to cleanse us from all unrighteousness"*. Acknowledgement of sin and confession are necessary to be forgiven and restored to fellowship with God (Rom. 10.10; 1 Jn. 1.9; 4.15). There is no implication in this passage that John is speaking of redeemed and sanctified believers who have been delivered from the power of sin, nor any indication that Christians are somehow holy and unholy at the same moment; or blameless and to be blamed in the same instant. This would be as absurd as referring to someone as a "truthful liar", an "honest thief", a "harmless pedophile," or a "holy fornicator".

The defense lawyers for sin charge or insinuate that those who teach against "sinning religion" are guilty of hypocrisy or otherwise of ignorantly exalting human nature by bestowing upon men an undue honor and power. They simply don't believe that native depravity, inbred sin, which gives rise to the commission of actual sins, can be eradicated or fully cleansed by faith in Christ[52]; and thus, they disparage and degrade, either wittingly or unwittingly, Christ's salvific work in redemption, regeneration, and sanctification.

This is the crux of the argument of Calvinists and Protestants in general over against believers in the Wesleyan-holiness tradition of faith; for the latter believe that, in teaching against the commission of sin, they are rather exalting the power of God's grace to fully cleanse men's souls and thus to make men free from sin--- *"[saving] them to the uttermost"* (Heb. 7.25). In proclaiming the "Good News" of being *"made free from sin"*, they open the door for the *"reign of righteousness"* and close the door against the *"reign of sin and death"* (Rom. 5.17, 21).

Holiness believers assert further that the power of Christ in salvation can keep a believer in a state of consecrated grace and blamelessness before the Lord (1 Cor. 1.8; Phil. 2.15; 3.6; Col. 1.22; 1 Thess. 5.23; 2 Pet. 3.14; Jude 24). Even the celebrated Augustine declared as much while serving as bishop in north Africa in the late fourth- and early fifth century, going so far to say

---

[52] The notes on 1 Jn. 3.6-9 in ex. ed. Spiros Zodhiates, and Warren Baker, managing editor, *The Hebrew-Greek Key Word Study Bible* (Chattanooga, TN: AMG Publishers, second revised edition, 1990) are typical. The author of the "Study Helps" denies that inbred sin, "the sin nature", can be eradicated, and emphasizes that though a believer "may fall into sin" yet his "eternal salvation is not affected".

that to deny the possibility of moral and spiritual perfection is to call the grace of God into question. We maintain therefore that complete deliverance from sin is the only God-honoring and truly Scriptural view. Christian perfection was in fact taught and maintained by most of the Early Church Fathers. Clement of Alexandria (c. 150-215) is typical: "He who holds conversation with God must have his soul immaculate and pure, without stain. It is essential to have made himself perfectly good". Again, "As I conceive it, sanctity is perfect pureness of mind, deeds, thoughts, and words". And again, "Abstinence from sins is not sufficient for perfection, unless a person also assumes the work of righteousness---activity in doing good".[53]

Accordingly, to hold that men can live above sin exalts God's grace and His salvific work in Christ, not man's abilities nor any innate goodness in fallen man. This is plainly the point in the teachings and prayers of the apostles, and of all the inspired writers in the Bible. *"Now unto him that is able to do exceeding abundantly above all that we ask or think, according to the power that worketh in us, unto him be glory in the church by Christ Jesus throughout all ages, world without end. Amen"* (Eph. 3.20-21).

In stating our case against "sinning religion", however, we endeavor to avoid any implication or notion of absolute perfection, or of leaving the impression that Christians cannot sin. We readily admit that a Christian may stumble and commit a willful act of sin; and, in fact, that the great majority of professing Christians do commit sins, especially in these very last days. For we are living in a promiscuous age; a time in which multitudes of believers are *"falling away"* from the true faith of the Gospel, being pulled by the powerful current of worldliness and the spirit of antichrist as

---

[53] David W. Bercot, ed. *A Dictionary of Early Christian Beliefs* (Peabody, Mass. Hendrickson Publishers, Inc. 1998), p. 507.

predicted by the apostles and inspired writers in the New Testament (Acts 20.29; 2 Thess. 2.3-12; Heb. 6.4-12; 1 Jn. 2.18-29; 4.1-6). But this is the whole point: it is not normal for Christians to sin; it is rather a sign of laxity, indifference, and abnormality; it is the prophetic mark of *"departing from the faith"* and *"falling away"* from holiness and consecration in the Holy Spirit (1 Tim. 4.1-3; 2 Tim. 3.1-8). For God has *"called us . . . unto holiness"* (1 Thess. 4.7), and commanded us to *"Be ye holy, for I am holy"* (1 Pet. 1.16; see also Lu. 1.74-75; Rom. 6.19, 22; 2 Cor. 7.1; Eph. 4.24; 1 Thess. 3.13; 1 Tim. 2.15; Titus 2.3; Heb. 12.10, 14); and He has provided the dynamic means for holy living in Christ, who is also able to *"save us to the uttermost"* and to *"keep us from falling"*.

In view of the mass of Scriptural evidence against any justification for "sinning religion", we not only utterly deny that Christians must habitually sin or sin on a regular basis but assert that they do not have to sin at all; and that purity and holiness should be the aim of every child of God. It is true that in some instances the term *sin* is used in the present tense denoting grammatically a continuous action. Such is the case, for example, in 1 Jn. 3.9; but there is no theological implication that this is merely a censure against habitual sin or the regular practice of sin; rather the implication is that one who is born of God and remains consecrated in the Spirit will not and cannot commit sin. It is the same as saying in other words what the apostle Paul says in Rom. 6.2: *"How shall we, that are dead to sin, live any longer therein?"* And again, *"For he that is dead is freed from sin"* (v. 7). This is not to say, however, that one cannot backslide or apostatize, but rather that *"There is no condemnation to them which are in Christ Jesus, who walk not after the flesh, but after the Spirit"* (8.1). And again, *"Walk in the Spirit, and ye shall not fulfill the lusts of the flesh"* (Gal. 5.16). In other words, if one is loving and adoring God in his heart, he cannot sin: for such a state of grace prevents it!

In cases in which a saint might lapse in his consecration and stumbles and commits *a* sin, we do indeed have an advocate with the Father. In these cases, the true saint of God will immediately feel the weight of his transgression and ask for forgiveness with "godly sorrow" until he feels perfectly cleared of his offense and stands again blameless before the Lord. The apostle John addressed the possibility of this very scenario in the lives of believers, but only after first admonishing them to sin not at all. *"My little children, these things I write unto you, that ye sin not. And if any man sin, we have an advocate with the Father, Jesus Christ the righteous"* (1 Jn. 2.1). Note carefully, *"And if any man sin"* not "when any man sin". The verb here is in the aorist tense indicating a single action of sin, not habitual or continual sinning. The point is that if sin is committed at all among God's people it should be the exception, not the rule; indeed, a rare occasion always accompanied with shame, godly sorrow, and repentance.

Jesus warned about *"blind leaders of the blind"*, saying *"shall they not both fall into the ditch"?* (Mt. 15.14; Lu. 6.39). This was His word to the Jews that believed on Him. He warned them against the corrupt teachings of their leaders---the scribes and Pharisees---and rather taught them, *"If ye continue in my word, then are ye my disciples indeed; and ye shall know the truth, and the truth shall make you free.* Then He more plainly and pointedly stated, *"... I say unto you, whosoever committeth sin is the servant of sin. And the servant abideth not in the house for ever: but the Son abideth ever. If the Son therefore shall make you free, ye shall be free indeed"* (Jn. 8.34-36).

We see then that sin is abnormal for Christians, and that those who practice "sinning religion" will not always abide in God's house. For His house, the temple of the Lord, the church, is called to be holy! It is beautified with holiness. *"Holiness becometh thine house, O Lord, for ever"* (Ps. 93.5). And again, *"But upon mount Zion there shall be . . . holiness"* (Obadiah 17).

We may be sure that Christ is returning for a *"glorious church, not having spot, or wrinkle, or any such thing; but that it should be holy and without blemish"* (Eph. 5.27): a church that has been *"[sanctified and cleansed] with the washing of water by the word"* (v. 26). For *"we know that, when He shall appear, we shall be like Him; for we shall see Him as He is. And every man that hath this hope in Him purifieth himself, even as He is pure"* (1 Jn. 3.2-3).

Uncle Ben's Cough Syrup

We are reminded of the faithful pastor who proclaimed God's Word without compromise. His firm stance against sin and his straight forward preaching alarmed several of the prominent members of his liberal congregation, which prompted them to call a meeting with him to voice their objections. Boldly they said, "Pastor, we think you're too plain in your preaching about sin and corruption, particularly regarding our young people. We advise therefore that you should lighten up, and not be so plain and graphic in your sermons on sin." The pastor then removed a bottle off the shelf from behind his desk. The label said in bold letters, "Strychnine," and below was the word "poison" written in large red letters. The wise pastor then said to the group, "What you are asking of me would be like changing this label to say, *'Uncle Ben's Cough Syrup.'* This would be a great deception and probably cause some folks to become deathly sick and perhaps even cause some to die."

I once was lost in sin, but Jesus took me in,
And then a little light from heaven filled my soul;
It bathed my heart in love and wrote my named above,
And just a little talk with Jesus made me whole.

Conclusion

Sin is a dangerous and deadly enemy that should be taken with utmost seriousness and gravity. To be sure, some sins are more grievous and damaging than others; but all sin finally is destructive to the soul and eternally damning.

Our responsibility is to proclaim the plain truth about sin and its consequences. We must not modify or sugar-coat it. The problem with so-called "little sins" is that they don't stay little, and, in any case, all sin is of the same nature, and we know that no sin can enter heaven. *"And there shall in no wise enter into [heaven] anything that defiles, neither whatsoever works abomination, or makes a lie"* (Rev. 21.27). Again, hear the words of the apostle as he beheld the apocalyptic vision of the end-times, and received the message from the mighty angel of God: *"For without [the city of God] are dogs, and sorcerers, and whoremongers, and murderers, and idolaters, and whosoever loves and makes a lie"* (Rev. 22.15). And again, *"And whosoever was not found written in the book of life was cast into the lake of fire"* (20.15).

138

INDEX OF BIBLICAL REFERENCES

Bibliography

Bercot, David W., *A Dictionary of Early Christian Beliefs: A Reference Guide to More Than 700 Topics Discussed by the Early Church Fathers* (Peabody, MA: Hendrickson Publishers, 1998).

Berkhof, Louis, *Systematic Theology* (Grand Rapids, MI: WM. B. Eerdmans Publishing Co. 1939, 1941, 1949).

Brockett, Henry E., *Scriptural Freedom from Sin* (Nicholasville, KY: Schmul Publishing Co., 1980).

Burgess, Stanley M. and Maas, Eduard M. Van Der, *The New International Dictionary of Pentecostal and Charismatic Movements* (Grand Rapids, MI: Zondervan Publishing House, 2002).

Burges, Stanley M. and McGee, Gary B., *Dictionary of Pentecostal and Charismatic Movements* (Grand Rapids, MI: Zondervan Publishing House, 1988).

Calvin, John, *Institutes of The Christian Religion* (Grand Rapids, MI: Eerdmans Publishing Co., reprint 1983).

Clarke, Adam, *Christian Theology* (Salem, OH: Schmul Publishing Co., Inc., reprint 1990).

Clarke, Adam, *Commentary* (6 Vols., New York: Abingdon Press, 1832).

Cox, Leo George, *John Wesley's Concept of Sin* (Salem, OH: Schmul Publishing Col, 2002).

Dryden, John, *The Harvard Classics Virgil's Aeneid* (Danbury, CT: Grolier Enterprises Corp., 1982 of 1909 ed.).

Findlater, John, *Perfect Love: A Study of Wesley's View of the Ideal Christian Life* (Salem, OH: Schmul Publishing Co., 1985).

Fletcher, John, *Fletcher on Perfection* (Nicholasville, KY: Schmul Publishing Co., reprint 2000).

Foster, R. S., *Objections To Calvinism As It Is* (Nicholasville, KY: Schmul Publishing Co., 1998).

Gregory, Benjamin, *Perfect in Christ Jesus* (Salem, OH: Schmul Publishing Co., 1994).

Hastings, Adrian, *The Oxford Companion to Christian Thought* (Oxford: University Press, 2000).

Henry, Matthew, *Matthew Henry's Commentary On the Whole Bible* (6 Vols.; Peabody, MA: Hendrickson Publishers, 1991).

Hills, A. M., *Fundamental Christian Theology* (Salem, OH: Schmul Publishing Co., reprint. 1980).

Hodge, Charles, *Systematic Theology* (1 Vol.; abridged ed., Grand Rapids, MI: Baker Book House, reprint 1988).

Hodge, Charles, *Systematic Theology* (3 Vols.; reprint.; Grand Rapids, MI: Wm. B. Eerdmans Publishing Co., reprint 1979).

Marsh, E. G., *The Old Man* (Nicholasville, KY: Schmul Publishing Co., 2011).

McBrien, Richard P., *The HarperCollins Encyclopedia of Catholicism* (New York, NY: Harper Collins Publishers Inc., 1995).

Mead, Frank S., *Handbook of Denominations In The United States* (Nashville: Abingdon Press, 1951).

Miley, John, *Systematic Theology* (2 Vols., New York: Eaton & Mains, 1894).

Nichols, James and Nichols, William *The Works of James Arminius The London Edition* (3 Vols.; Grand Rapids, MI: Baker Book House, 1986).

Pearlman, Myer, *Knowing The Doctrines Of The Bible* (Springfield, MO: Gospel Publishing House, 1937).

Robertson, Archibald Thomas, *Word Pictures In The New Testament* (6 Vols.; Grand Rapids, MI: 1930).

Ruth, C. W., *Entire Sanctification In Daily Life* (Nicholasville, KY: Schmul Publishing Co., reprint 2010).

Sauls, Ned D., *Pentecostal Doctrines A Wesleyan Approach* (Dunn, NC: The Heritage Press, 1979).

Shedd, William G. T., *Dogmatic Theology* (3 Vols.; Nashville, TN: Thomas Nelson Publishers, 1980, reprint.).

Smith, Timothy L., *Whitefield & Wesley On The New Birth* (Grand Rapids, MI: Francis Asbury Press of Zondervan Publishing House, 1986).

Strong, A. H., *Systematic Theology* (Valley Forge, PA: Judson Press, 1907).

Taylor, Richard S., *A Right Conception of Sin* (Nicholasville, KY: Schmul Publishing Co., 2002).

Taylor, Richard S., *The Scandal of Pre-Forgiveness* (Nicholasville, KY: Schmul Publishing Co., 1993).

Tenny, Merrill C., *The Zondervan Pictorial Encyclopedia of the Bible* (5 Vols., Grand Rapids, MI: Zondervan Publishing House 1975).

152

Tyson, John R., *Charles Wesley On Sanctification: A Biographical and Theological Study* (Salem, OH: Schmul Publishing Co., 1992).

Wakefield, Samuel, *A Complete System of Christian Theology or, A Concise, Comprehensive, and Systematic View of the Evidences, Doctrines, Morals, and Institutions of Christianity* (Nicholasville, KY: Schmul Publishing Co., reprint 1985).

Wesley, John, *A Plain Account of Christian Perfection As Believed and Taught By The Reverend Mr. John Wesley 1725-1777* (Nicholasville, KY: Schmul Publishing Co., reprint 2015).

Wesley, John, *Calvinism Calmly Considered* (Nicholasville, KY: Schmul Publishing Co., reprint 2001).

Wesley, John, *New Testament: Translation and Notes in Modern English,* (2 Vols.; Nicholasville, KY: Schmul Publishing Co., 2012).

Wesley, John, *The Doctrine Of Original Sin According To Scripture, Reason and Experience* (Salem, OH: Schmul Publishing Co., reprint 1999).

Wesley, John, *The Works of John Wesley* (15 Vols.; Grand Rapids: Baker Book House: reprint 1984 of 1872 ed.).

Wesley, John and Clarke, Adam, *The Entire New Testament on Holiness A Concise Verse by Verse Commentary* (Nicholasville, KY: Schmul Publishing Co., reprint 2001).

Wiley, Orton H., *Christian Theology* (3 Vols.; Kansas City, KS: Nazarene Publishing House, 1941).

Youngblood, Ronald, F., gen. ed., *New Illustrated Bible Dictionary* (Nashville: Thomas Nelson, 1995).

Zodhiates, Spiros, and Baker, Warren, mg. ed., *The Hebrew-Greek Key Word Study Bible* (Chattanooga, TN: AMG Publishers, second rev. ed., 1990).

94816559R00089

Made in the USA
Columbia, SC
05 May 2018